Crowdsourcing, Constructing and Collaborating

Crowdsourcing, Constructing and Collaborating

Methods and Social Impacts of Mapping the World Today

Edited by

Siddharth Peter de Souza,
Nida Rehman and Saba Sharma

BLOOMSBURY
NEW DELHI • LONDON • OXFORD • NEW YORK • SYDNEY

BLOOMSBURY INDIA
Bloomsbury Publishing India Pvt. Ltd
Second Floor, LSC Building No. 4, DDA Complex, Pocket C – 6 & 7,
Vasant Kunj, New Delhi 110070

BLOOMSBURY, BLOOMSBURY ACADEMIC INDIA and the Diana logo are trademarks of Bloomsbury Publishing Plc

First published in India 2021
This edition published 2021

Bloomsbury Academic
An imprint of Bloomsbury Publishing Plc

ISBN: HB: 978-93-88630-43-6; eBook: 978-93-88630-45-0

2 4 6 8 10 9 7 5 3 1

Typeset in Minion Pro by Manipal Technologies Limited
Printed and bound in India by Replika Press Pvt. Ltd.

For Alma and the next generation who will map our world.

CONTENTS

PART III: FEMINIST INTERVENTIONS

PART IV: CIVIC ENGAGEMENTS

ACKNOWLEDGEMENTS

We would like to begin by thanking the contributors to this volume who believed in and engaged with this project, and showed great commitment to see it to its completion—Lena Weber, Leah Temper, Daniela Del Bene, Hend Alhinnawi, Taha Kass-Hout, Jan Böhm, Rob Shepard, Ahmad Barclay, Joumana al Jabri, Farah Shash, Angie Abdelmonem, Noora Flinkman and Juliana Guarany da Cunha Santos, Sumit Arora, Sandhya Christabel D'Souza, Dheeman Ghosh and Rebecca Rumbul. We are grateful that that they invested their time in the book and were willing to share experiences from their wonderful projects, the milestones they have achieved, and the challenges they have faced, openly and with the ambition of building a community of knowledge.

Thank you especially to Nooreen Reza for her commitment to the book and to Intolerance Tracker. We would like to thank Vaibhav Bhawsar and Somnath Ray for supporting Intolerance Tracker with Timescape and helping the project off the ground. Anne Alexander, Emma Mawdsley and Bhaskar Vira from the University of Cambridge have been supporters of the project from its inception and we are grateful for their guidance and advice.

We would like to thank Shannon Mattern for her thoughtful Afterword, and for her enthusiasm and encouragement about the project.

R. Chandra Sekhar at Bloomsbury has been instrumental in seeing this project through, we thank him for his editorial advice and for ensuring the editorial process has been smooth and efficient. We are also grateful to Shreya Chakraborti at Bloomsbury for her help with the editorial process and to the two anonymous reviewers for their helpful comments on the manuscript.

Siddharth would like to thank Nida and Saba for being two wonderful collaborators throughout this process, and for making this project an exciting and meaningful experience for him. He would like to thank his parents Peter and Ligia and his sisters Gayatri and Roshni and Dhulari for their banter, chat and brainstorming whenever called upon and to Pravesh and Rashmi, his in-laws, for their encouragement in seeing this through.

Nida is very grateful to Siddharth and Saba for their energy, enthusiasm and intelligence in this collaboration. She is also thanks her family in Pakistan, Colombia and the US for their support, Daniel Cardoso Llach for his never-ending advice, encouragement and love, and Alma for her company through the final stages of this project and beyond.

Saba would like to thank her parents, in-laws, and Ambika, Vasav and Sarab for their support and company. Nida and Siddharth have been the best possible collaborators to work with.

INTRODUCTION

Siddharth Peter de Souza, Nida Rehman and Saba Sharma

The last decade has seen a significant rise in the use of internet-based mapping techniques to foster social change. Map-makers and citizens around the world—from local groups to large-scale transnational communities—use online mapping and collaborating platforms to hold governments accountable, to fill gaps when infrastructural and municipal services are fragmented, to call attention to a variety of issues that impact everyday lives such as sexual or political violence, environmental injustice or corruption and to make visible social and political processes and events that might be otherwise hidden or overlooked. Yet, despite the proliferation of crowdsourced, participatory and data visualisation platforms and despite significant media and scholarly coverage of the types and uses of online maps and their social and political potentials or impacts, there is a surprising dearth of critical reflection on the actual experiences of building and sustaining such platforms. In this collection of edited essays and interviews, *Crowdsourcing, Constructing and Collaborating* uniquely brings together individuals and groups directly involved in a range of projects from around the world, to critically reflect on the tactics, methods and challenges of crowdsourcing and data visualization, as well as other online mapping tools, to instigate social, environmental and political change. Addressing a range of topical challenges, including corruption, sexual harassment, political violence and environmental conflict in diverse geographic contexts, these projects show how participatory digital media have become crucial components of journalistic, scholarly and activist practices. This book shifts the conversation from maps to the practices of map-making.

From Maps to Map-making Practices

Crowdsourcing, Constructing and Collaborating builds on our work on Intolerance Tracker, which we established in 2016 in collaboration with the online storytelling platform Timescape. Intolerance Tracker was a response to the increasing frequency of social, political, ethnic and gender violence at different scales in South Asia, and an effort to consolidate media reports of instances of violence and hate crimes in order to understand systemic and underlying trends of intolerance in the region and across national boundaries. For this book, we gathered individuals involved in setting up and working with other online map-making platforms—the founders and members of I Paid A Bribe, Environmental Justice Atlas, HarassMap, Intolerance Tracker, Visualizing Palestine, Missing Maps, FemMap, Placing Segregation, Fix My Street and Humanitarian Tracker—to discuss the values, methods and experiences of building similar tools for activism, information dissemination, networking and solidarity. Together the different projects represent a range of themes, approaches and objectives that include archiving and documenting contested territories and processes (Visualizing Palestine/Palestine Open Maps, Placing Segregation, Intolerance Tracker), the participatory and urgent mapping of humanitarian and environmental crises (Humanitarian Tracker, EJAtlas, Missing Maps), civic and community initiatives (I Paid a Bribe, FixMyStreet) and feminist and social interventions (FemMap, HarassMap). While the themes are distinct, what ties together the different reflections from the projects is that they are driven by the map-makers themselves. The projects in this book represent a diverse set of issues—environmental injustices, civil and military conflicts, corruption, sexual harassment, everyday manifestations of hate and intolerance and more. They feature contributions from across different parts of the globe, with some maps concentrating on local issues, and others adopting global or regional approaches. Each is unique from the perspective of the context they embed themselves in, enabling us to see a wide cross-section of geographies.

The book provides readers with grounded and reflexive evaluations of the methodological and ethical challenges that have come with the use of participatory and other digital tools in education, crisis responsiveness, media reportage and government functioning. In bringing together this diverse group of contributors who build, maintain and use online map-making platforms, we hope to extend the grounded and collaborative ethos of their practices, and to build a mutually enriching conversation amongst the different contributors, as well as with readers. The book includes essays and interviews as a means to reflect on the practice of using online maps and to provide a more conversational format bridging advocacy and academia. By introducing an element of dialogue to the reflections, we hope to further enhance the voices of these map-makers.

We argue that in order to advance the potential of crowdsourcing and other forms of online mapping, there is a need to move beyond technologically deterministic narratives of visibility or citizen participation, to more reflective accounts about these practices. By drawing from projects around the world, the volume reflects on a variety of experiences—from online mapping that takes place in specific, localised contexts (for instance, documenting street harassment in Egypt or creating maps to visualise present-day Palestine) to other maps that link different parts of the world through their representation on a common platform (for instance, hate crimes in various South Asian countries, or environmental conflicts across the world). We examine online mapping as one aspect of a newer and increasingly expanding online platform and a crucial aspect of activism and mobilisation. The book thus seeks to build a community of practice amongst groups that are directly engaged in different approaches to citizen participation and learning through online cartography.

In the remainder of this introductory essay, we discuss three key aspects of online mapping explored in the chapters. First, we look at online mapping as a form of storytelling in the digital sphere and the importance of storytelling in particular as a component of advocacy. Second, we review the constructed nature of maps and the ways in which online mapping makes visible the creators and consumers of maps. Third, we look at the collaborative and collective nature of these forms of map-making and the ways in which their authors conceptualise questions of participation, the multiplicity and diversity of data and interdisciplinarity.

Building Stories Through Maps

In this book, a crucial lens through which we engage with online mapping is by looking at map-making as a form of storytelling. Far from neutral or objective forms of collating data, maps have always served to tell particular stories—about their authors, about states and the governing of territories and populations, or about the processes of the natural world or the universe at large. The emergence of thematic maps in the

19th century, used as visual tools to present specific kinds of information around a theme (often to do with governing populations), in particular, highlight the status of maps as a form of argument (Schulten 2012). Maps were a key part of the discourse of imperial geopolitical thought, with visual representations of empires serving as a key tool to justify the expansion of control, such as the work of British geographer and politician Halford Mackinder (1904), who used maps as a means to argue for British expansion into the Asian landmass. Maps have continued to be used in this way in contemporary geopolitical manoeuvrings. Samuel Huntington's (in)famous *The Clash of Civilizations* thesis uses a map to illustrate (and subsequently justify as self-evident) the presence of distinct 'civilisations' across the world, and the inevitability of conflict between them (Huntington 1993). Similarly, American military geostrategist Thomas Barnett visualises *The Pentagon's New Map* (reproduced in Dittmer and Sharp 2014) as dividing the world into areas of 'the Core' and 'the Gap', which are used to justify American military expansion to areas that form part of the 'Gap' in 'globalization's ozone hole'. In each instance, maps are part of the argument of power, deployed by powerful actors.

The history of maps often presents them as easily readable devices that are a universal graphic language, existing in multiple cultural contexts; however, they are more often open to interpretation, rife with ambiguities and not always easily translatable (Harley 1987). While traditional cartography presented maps as a fixed and objective form of knowledge, they have increasingly been deconstructed as a representation and instrument of power (Harley 1989). The purpose of this book is not only to continue in that tradition of critique, and view maps as subjective forms of knowledge production, but also to explore how this particular method of creating knowledge is a form of storytelling in the digital sphere. Given the increasing focus on everyday experience in a variety of approaches—academic and otherwise—to social phenomena, stories are an effective means of producing knowledge through their ability to connect personal narratives to wider political, social and cultural contexts (Cameron 2012).

Each mapping project in this book adopts a thematic approach to map-making to tell a particular story from a part of the world, or across regional and transnational geographies. Often these stories collect information that already exists in the public sphere (such as Intolerance Tracker or Placing Segregation), but putting them on a map gives the data a new narrative, in a more accessible visual form. Other maps generate new data around a theme (as in the case of HarassMap and I Paid a Bribe that highlight issues of sexual harassment and corruption in governance, respectively), and attempt to tie these individual experiences into a broader understanding of a social phenomenon, made more current and topical through the constant updating of this narrative with incoming data. The stories, like the maps, acquire a dynamic character as a result.

Online mapping as storytelling links to an emergent form of digital storytelling, in which cartographic language is just one medium. A variety of online media, such as written narratives, photographs, participatory blogs (Alexandra 2008; Burgess 2006; Vivienne; Burgess 2013) are all part of efforts to democratise knowledge production. Digital storytelling has the potential to strengthen a more democratic narrative (Couldry 2008), by creating means to produce 'bottom-up' narratives. Digital narratives have been used effectively as forms of advocacy, in highlighting human rights issues, using personal digital narratives (especially visual narratives) as a way of making broader public claims about rights abuses, for instance (Gregory et al. 2006). While contemporary mapping as an emancipatory exercise is an important development (and the main theme of this book), it is important to keep in mind that it can also become a tool of exclusion. An example of this is crime-mapping software in use by police departments across the US, which creates a 'landscape of danger' that reinforces gender and racial stereotypes in the name of safety and places the responsibility of crime prevention on individuals rather than the state (Wallace 2009). Similar to what is true of traditional cartography, the story depends on the storyteller.

Online mapping ties together personal narratives in a particular visual language, using the familiar language of cartography and combining it with the more recent trend of aggregating personal narratives using digital mediums. It can become a tool of counter-cartography, similar to how mapping as a tool has been re-appropriated by less powerful groups to present counter-claims and alternative territorial imaginations (see for example kollectiv orangotango+ 2018). As with all forms of storytelling, online mapping—especially where data is crowdsourced, compiled by volunteers, or aggregated from diverse sources—is subject to questions of consistency and accuracy of the story it tells. But such forms of mapping, in revealing or making explicit their inherently subjective nature, only serve to illustrate how conventional maps are also essentially partial and reflect a particular lens in representing places, even if they seem to stem from a single, authoritative and often anonymous source (Dodge and Kitchin 2013). Mapping has always been inherently political, and this politics is made more visible through the explicit use of mapping in forms of advocacy, as is the case for the contributions in this volume.

Constructing Maps to Project, Inquire and Collect

It is hardly controversial that the most ubiquitous modes of representing global and territorial space—from the 1569 Mercator projection to its contemporary reincarnations in Google Maps[1]—naturalise their own graphic distortions and reinforce a view of the world that is neutral, authoritative and stable. As James Corner (1999, p. 216) describes, 'mappings are constructed from a set of internal instruments, codes, techniques and conventions' that circumscribe their possible interpretations and instrumentalisations. As scholars, cartographers and artists have widely shown, rather than conveying universal truths or unchanging facts about space and society, maps—and the ways in which their graphic languages, rules, units, scales and data are constructed and presented—imbed, reinforce or amplify their makers' biases and aspirations (Corner 1999; Wood and Fels 2008; Foster 2014). In other words, the visual, graphic, data gathering and analytical tools used to construct maps shape their interpretive possibilities—and are thus central to their utility as instruments of empire, militarism, surveillance, territorial dispossession and other forms of state, extra-state and non-state power and violence (See for example Peluso 1995; Scott 1999; Cosgrove 1999). In this book, we are interested in exploring how map-making practices and techniques, particularly through online and collaborative means, offer an alternative range of possibilities to reimagine, reorient or disrupt claims of neutrality, authority and authorial stability. We focus on practices deploying logics of construction and representation that make explicit their projective, inquisitive and collective ethos, and through which they seek to reveal, question or overturn particular structures of power. Together the online platforms featured in this book use different graphic conventions and techniques of map-making to variously reimagine and project, create new ways to see and understand reality and shape collective and plural rather than singular views.

The long-standing associations (and often acceptance) of the documentary neutrality of maps is upheld by cartographic conventions, as well as by their increasing ubiquity in everyday lives (Mattern 2015). Yet, we know that 'maps are not copies, (but) projections' (Ulrich and McCarthy 2014, p. 6) in at least two different ways. First, as Tom McCarthy notes, drawing from J.A. Steer's 1927 book *Introduction to the Study of Map Projections*, maps represent—indeed translate—formations from the earth's spherical surface (and other physical realities) onto two-dimensional paper (or screen). In the process of attaining legibility through translation and abstraction, conventions of cartographic projection, with the Mercator projection being the most ubiquitous, necessarily operate by stretching, compressing or warping spatial areas, as well as through 'selection, omission, isolation, distance and codification' (Corner 1999, p. 215). But maps also project in other ways. In his seminal essay 'The Agency of Mapping', Corner (1999) argues that spatial planners and designers (and we can extend that to activists, scholars, artists and citizens in general) may engage mappings not as neutral objects—representing some kind of truth about space—but as cultural artefacts through which to reimagine and recreate the world (see also Duxbury et al. 2018). The projective impulse is particularly evident in some of the contributed projects in this collection such as HarassMap, Humanitarian Tracker and FixMyStreet, in which the pinpointing of particular, geolocated incidences—of sexual harassment, military conflicts and war crimes and municipal problems—is tied to mechanisms for action and amelioration. For example, HarassMap's homepage—in addition to presenting the cartographic aggregation of incidences of harassment in Egypt and instructions for reporting them—links users directly to a range of resources for support and mechanisms to inform research and take action on the issue of sexual harassment.

The creative and projective possibilities of digital mapping platforms also rely strongly on their capacity to act as forms of enquiry rather than as reifications of authority and hegemony. Working outside of and against the 'God's-view,' map-makers—artists, activists, scholars and designers—increasingly create new methods and ways of knowing the world. From everyday forms of orientation, navigation and narration, to possibilities for playful explorations and spatial 'drift' (Pinder 1996), to more radical practices of subversion and counter-cartography (Peluso 1995; Bhagat and Mogel, 2008; kollectiv orangotango+ 2018), such practices can visually reveal the spatial, social, environmental and political processes and relationships otherwise hidden or erased in official narratives of mainstream discourses. Through techniques of juxtaposition, excavation, layering, re-ordering, reorienting and pinpointing they can sharpen insights and open entirely new perspectives onto existing and ongoing events, and thus help to make or renew claims previously unheeded (Duxbury et al. 2015). The revelatory potential of online mapping is at the heart of projects such as Palestine Open Maps and Placing Segregation. The former deploys historic base maps, specifically 1940s survey maps of Palestine, first making them navigable and searchable, and then layering them with contemporary data about the presence—and destruction—of Palestinian settlements. This project thus directly confronts hegemonic narratives that question (and thus erase) the very existence of Palestinian lives and spaces in the region. Placing Segregation similarly utilises not only historic base maps but also historic census data, to visualise patterns of racial and class-based segregation in American cities.

Another important dimension of online mapping practices and techniques is the challenge they present to the fixity of cartographic representations. Shannon Mattern (2015) suggests that, in bringing together different agents of mapping, multiple data-sets as well as a diverse range of users, contemporary forms of online map-making operate as media powerfully suited to destabilising singular views and perceptions of stability. In this regard, the use of crowd-mapping and participatory approaches, including the pioneering role of Open Street Maps, is particularly notable (Badger 2013). In highlighting the situatedness of sometimes very individual experiences and relationships 'pinned' and 'tagged' by individual users, these forms of distributed, iterative and processual mapping draw attention to the flexibility, contingency and heterogeneity of collective experience (Kitchin et al. 2013). It is exactly the aggregation of individual experiences and events that allows projects such as the Environmental Justice Atlas (EJAtlas), HarassMap, I Paid a Bribe and Humanitarian Tracker to challenge the stability of singular narratives. The individual case studies featured within the EJAtlas provide both meticulously documented information on particular cases of environmental injustice and mobilisation, as well as a more zoomed-out view of the world through the lens of environmental conflict. The fine-grained categories of information—including sources of conflict, forms and agents of mobilisation, political outcomes, health impacts as well as the inclusion of additional media and voices—shape a contingent and unfolding rather than a static view of each case. The graphics of the HarassMap website balance the cartographic view, indicating the numbers of reported sexual harassment cases in different areas, with clear mechanisms to report incidents or interventions, thus emphasising the collective construction of the map. In a slightly different vein, the homepage of Intolerance Tracker defaults to the Google Earth satellite image as a base map to deemphasise the stability of otherwise highly rigid and securitised national boundaries, and highlight instead the transnational nature of rising hate and intolerance in the region.

Collaboration and Participation

In highlighting collaboration as a crucial aspect of mapping practice in the projects in this book, we recognise the nature of participatory knowledge production, and also the engagement with communities who contribute and are represented by these maps. Collaboration, as a principle, is central to the design of these projects, because it ensures that narratives framed on these platforms are shaped through processes that attempt to be more democratic in collecting, recording and presenting data (Warner 2015; Norheim-Hagtun and Meier 2010).

Connecting closely with communities in mapping issues related to environmental justice, corruption, humanitarian work or hate crimes enables these maps to draw on rich ecologies of knowledge that are based in lived experiences, and also with the informational contexts of the affected communities by virtue of the sources they use. This marks a distinction with traditional mapping projects, wherein—rather than technical considerations of experts who could provide more normative readings of issues such as housing segregation or sexual harassment—these maps privilege experiences as empirical insights into ways of seeing the world.

In the case of FixMyStreet, for example, such lived experiences can also have a technical value of their own. Mapping devices allow residents to report difficulties they face, whether in terms of a garbage disposal or damage to roads, which are then used to provide actionable data to help local organisations and municipal councils respond to the needs of its residents. In the case of Humanitarian Tracker, a complex set of issues, tracking human rights violations, understanding the outbreak of diseases and providing data on safe routes for humanitarian aid workers, are mapped. In doing so, this intervention provides a grounded view of a dynamic conflict environment and allows for more efficient and targeted intervention aimed at ensuring greater impact. Both these projects are collaborative, not just in their collection of data but also in terms of how they are then utilised by different agencies in order to take action.

Shifting the ownership of the narratives to being shaped and influenced by a plurality of voices, rather than being made invisible or co-opted through technicalities (Chari 2017), is a critical departure that attempts to make the mapping in these projects more reflective. These projects seek to represent less mainstream issues, make marginalised voices heard and provide a counter to linear narratives on a variety of issues. Many projects make explicit their ambitions to capture erasures prevalent in dominant cartographic sources, and also reflect upon the difficulties of sometimes matching such aspirations. Visualising Palestine and Placing Segregation, for example, use historical maps to provide a better sense of how narratives have been shaped over time, and how using archives can be a way of 'mapping back' to demonstrate the hegemonies that have emerged in both the narration and reflection through mapping devices in contemporary times (Chari 2017).

Through collaboration and participatory processes, these mapping exercises aim to move away from top-down approaches towards more grounded experiences that empower users to report on particular issues. (Mapping For Rights n.d.). In this way, participation in the mapping process is not passive or taken for granted, but users take on an important as researchers in terms of their knowledge and expertise. I Paid a Bribe, which sheds light on forms of everyday bureaucratic corruption in India and the ways in which they affect the everyday lives of people, and EJAtlas, which maps environmental conflicts and marginalisation around them, are examples of how resistances and lived experiences can be recorded and studied. In doing so, these projects also highlight the powers that underlie more statist forms of information dissemination and the kinds of exclusions and inclusions that take place as a result of these structures of knowledge (Mesquita 2018).

In addition to the transition from top-down mapping to more bottom-up processes, online mapping as a process is also dynamic (Halder and Michel 2018). Whereas traditional map-making can be seen as a process that once completed produces a fixed landscape of the world, online mapping makes that process intrinsically iterative. Iteration exists both as a design element and also as a political consideration. The mapping projects capture issues such as humanitarian work, which are constantly evolving, very often under-reported and typified by a lack of data. What these online maps provide are narratives that are constantly changing. In the instance of Intolerance Tracker, while the categories for capturing incidents were pre-assigned for aspects such as religion, gender and caste-based violence, there was nothing to correctly capture government crackdowns on civil society, an increasingly frequent occurance in the region. Part of the aim of building an online map was also the assumption that the categories to capture different instances of intolerance would not be rigid, but instead would respond to the data as it emerged. As a result, the process of categorisation was subject to change and review. This is one example of how mapping narratives can be influenced and transformed by the empirical insights emerging from the field.

Interdisciplinarity and diversity are key aspects of the mapping projects, which bring together expertise from those who are trained in geography, design, sociology, law, coding among others and between researchers, activists, social entrepreneurs, as well as ordinary citizens and users. As a result, the maps have different functions. There are times the maps are presented as illustrations of a larger project, while at other times they act as technical or social services for a wider community. The functions of the maps are the confluence of interests in the collaboration. They often play many roles, and herein also lies the flexibility of such projects.

The other value of investigating collaboration is the role it plays in community building. At one level the map-making process can be seen as democratising, as it introduces new voices. At another level, these projects themselves are devices to build communities where there is an opportunity for collaboration, solidarity and belonging. FemMap and HarassMap are two such examples, where the former explicitly tries to connect feminist projects across the world, and the latter aims to highlight and challenge sexual harassment. Through building a mapping platform they create a dialogue between different participants and see their maps as a form of sharing and solidarity.

However, while collaboration is seen as an ambition in many projects, and working with different communities is seen as a way to democratise knowledge production, many projects reflect a mismatch between aspiration and reality. Some argue, for example, that while democratisation is an aim, it is important that we remain attentive to how mapping projects often create new forms of power structures and elites, who can access such technologies and become gatekeepers who then decide on alternative, but not necessarily democratic, ways of seeing the world (Brandusescu; Sieber and Jochems 2016; Givoni 2016).

In This Volume

Following this introduction, the book is divided into four sections reflecting the different themes explored in the chapters—mapping crises, contested territories, feminist interventions and civic engagements. The chapters appear in two formats—essays and interviews. While the essays represent a more conventional format in which authors directly reflect on their experiences, with some of our participants we chose the more conversational and collaborative interview format to discuss the projects. In a book that focuses on the collaborative nature of map-making, dialogues seemed as relevant a method to explore the themes alongside the essays. The long-form interviews in this book bridge academic and journalistic approaches, such that they are shorter and more informal than academic texts, but longer and more reflective than a news interview. Here, we briefly explore the contributions in the volume and the broad themes that they cover.

An important function of online mapping has been to create a dynamic space to map different forms of crises and the responses to them, especially by those who have been engaged with the issues long-term. The first contribution , in chapter 1, is from the global mapping project and database known as Environmental Justice Atlas (or EJAtlas, for short), which serves not just as a map of global environmental conflicts, but also a platform for international networking and scholar-activist analysis. EJAtlas is built on co-produced knowledge and offers a tangible example of issues of political and academic rigour that emerge in a public political ecology project.

A different form of crisis is mapped in the Humanitarian Tracker project discussed in chapter 2, which uses crowd-mapping to respond to political conflict situations on the ground. Through a case study of the work carried out by the organisation in Syria, the project offers insights into how citizen empowerment can play a major role in development work post and during a conflict. These include detecting disturbances in different regions, maintaining and providing updated information on crises and for policy interventions.

Another initiative focussed on crisis mapping is the Missing Maps project, a collaboration between Médecins Sans Frontières/Doctors Without Borders (MSF), American and British Red Cross and Humanitarian OpenStreetMap Team (HOT), which is the subject of chapter 3. In making mapping crucial aspects of responding to disasters and emergencies, the team grapples with making maps of parts of the world often ignored by commercial interests and big companies. As many of the stories shared from the project show us, many parts of the world often lose out on aid and relief work simply because they are not visible on a map.

In addition to citizen participation, some forms of online mapping have also adopted forms of archiving and working with archives as a means of highlighting the contested nature of territories. Chapter 4 on Placing Segregation explores questions of housing segregation and socioeconomic disparities across 19th century American cities through a series of fully interactive maps and scholarly interpretations derived from the census data geolocated at the household level. Built for public audiences, the digital-map exhibit gives viewers direct access to geolocated census information for each available family in the years 1860 and 1870 for select US cities, providing searching and querying tools to enable public to ask research questions in a spatial environment.

Chapter 5 on Intolerance Tracker looks at the documentation and archiving of incidents of intolerance in South Asia, and how such a resource can be used to not only build a database of stories that get lost in the 24-hour news cycle, but also as a tool for advocacy and monitoring of various stakeholders. The chapter presents some of the lessons learnt in conceptualising intolerance, standardising and categorising forms of violence and presenting trends across South Asian countries.

One of the most fascinating uses of archival maps is by Palestine Open Maps, presented in chapter 6, which looks towards bridging historical and present-day maps. This project makes visible the systematic erasure of Palestine from global geography, both by delving into historical maps from the 1930s and 1940s, as well as creating contemporary maps. The authors reflect on the key thrusts of the project—that the maps be digitised, open-sourced and navigable by anyone. Like other projects in this volume, they use maps to make a part of the world more visible.

Online maps have emerged as a dynamic way to represent contestations of public and civic space, by using cartography to represent issues that have until recently not necessarily been seen through a spatial lens. In recent times, one of the most visible contests has been over public space, and in particular, women's access to it. The HarassMap project, examined in chapter 7, seeks to change public beliefs and behaviours in Egypt, by addressing problematic public conceptions of sexual harassment and to get people to agree to intervene in sexual harassment incidents. It uses new data collected through its crowd-mapping platform to combat these stereotypes. HarassMap is a means through which to help people submit anonymous reports of their sexual harassment experiences. The platform acts as a type of online survey, in which women are able to provide various details of when and where an incident occurred, as well as describe the incident itself. Examining the origins and motivations of the project, the chapter also looks at the challenges of visualising sexual harassment through a map—for instance, the complexities of crowd-mapping, mobilising communities and making the initiative sustainable. Meanwhile, FemMap, presented in chapter 8, aspires to build solidarity among different organisations that work on feminist issues. It is designed to foster collaboration and connections between different platforms, such that there is an opportunity to learn and share from the lessons adopted by each project. This project is designed to ensure that there is less fragmentation among projects working on feminist concerns.

Channelling citizen participation is the aim of I Paid a Bribe, which uses a series of novel visual and analytic tools in order to provide insights into the presence of corruption in different departments providing public utility services to ordinary Indians. Through collaboration and cooperation, chapter 9 examines the potential of building a ground-up movement against institutional and retail corruption, as well as the challenges of using technologies to sustain the movement.

The mapping project FixMyStreet, examined in chapter 10, combines civic participation with facilitating connections within a government to find solutions. It is a platform that crowd sources reports of issues of broken civic infrastructure, and enabling a discussion by encouraging users to post follow-ups on how and whether issues are dealt with by local councils in the United Kingdom. Issues of who participates and from where are important dynamics that the team must try to monitor. Equally important is the backend relationship that the platform must cultivate with the UK councils, and essentially find a space within the bureaucratic silos of the state, to encourage more active citizen participation as well as state response.

Forms of online mapping, particularly those employing participatory and crowd-sourced methods, are becoming increasingly ubiquitous, and are widely lauded in popular and social media. The intention of this volume, however, is not to add to the celebratory chorus, nor to fetishise technological novelty of these forms of online mapping (see Guldi 2017). Instead, *Crowdsourcing, Constructing and Collaborating* is more interested in highlighting the underlying ideological and practical ethos of these projects, and how they are developed and used critically and reflectively to further particular social or political causes. As Shannon Mattern suggests in the afterword to this volume, this requires attention to the 'analogue' aspects of digital practices—the various forms of labour that go into collecting data, sustaining outreach practices and creating communities around shared concerns. The essays thus follow lines of enquiry about the methods to collaboratively build maps that reflect a plurality of voices and stories and do so by staying close to the contingent and changing empirical realities of particular places and processes rather than amplifying expert or top-down views. Together they bring attention to ongoing and dynamic social, political and environmental challenges while helping open pathways to resistance or action.

Through this book, we hope to engage map-makers, academics, practitioners, students and citizens around the world who are curious about and interested in the democratic potential of mapping, as well as about the range of thematic issues represented, including environmental and social justice; histories of territorial violence and spatial segregation or displacement; social, ethnic and gender violence; and everyday forms of corruption, harassment and civic fracturing among others. Bringing these voices together in a critical, collaborative and comparative framework we also hope that this book will offer possibilities for reorienting and reimagining the world through maps.

Note

1. Google Maps discontinued its use of the Mercator projection in 2018 for zoomed out views of the earth, while continuing to use it at the scale of local places (See Polanco Masa 2018).

References

Alexandra, D. 'Digital Storytelling as Transformative Practice: Critical Analysis and Creative Expression in the Representation of Migration in Ireland'. *Journal of Media Practice* 9, no. 2 (2008): 101–112.

Badger, Emily. 'Mapping the Growth of OpenStreetMap'. *CityLab* (blog). 14 March 2013. Accessed 23 April 2019. http://www.theatlanticcities.com/commute/2013/03/mapping-growth-openstreetmap/4982/

Barnett, T. 'The Pentagon's New Map' in *Geopolitics: An Introductory Reader*, edited by J. Dittmer and J. Sharp. Oxon; New York: Routledge, [2003] 2014.

Bhagat, A. and L. Mogel. *An Atlas of Radical Cartography*, Spl. Edition. Los Angeles, California: Journal of Aesthetics and Protest Press, 2008.

Brandusescu, Ana, Renée E. Sieber and Sylvie Jochems. 'Confronting the Hype: The Use of Crisis Mapping for Community Development'. *Convergence* 22, no. 6 (2016): 616–32.

Burgess, J. 'Hearing Ordinary Voices: Cultural Studies, Vernacular Creativity and Digital Storytelling'. *Continuum* 20, no. 2 (2006): 201–214.

Cameron, E. 'New Geographies of Story and Storytelling'. *Progress in Human Geography* 36, no. 5 (2012): 573–592.

Chari, Sunitha. 'Mapping Back: A Workshop on Counter Mapping Resource Conflicts on Indigenous Homelands'. *Transformations to Sustainability*. 4 December 2017. https://transformationstosustainability.org/magazine/mapping-back-workshop-counter-mapping-resource-conflicts-indigenous-homelands/

Corner, James. 'The Agency of Mapping: Speculation, Critique and Invention'. In *Mappings*, 213–52. London: Reaktion Books, 1999.

Cosgrove, Denis. *Mappings*. London: Reaktion Books, 1999.

Couldry, N. 'Mediatisation or Mediation? Alternative Understandings of the Emergent Space of Digital Storytelling'. *New Media & Society* 10, no. 3 (2008): 373–391.

Dodge, M. and R. Kitchin. 'Crowdsourced Cartography: Mapping Experience and Knowledge'. *Environment and Planning A: Economy and Space* 45, no. 1 (2013): 19–36.

Duxbury, Nancy, W.F. Garrett-Petts and Alys Longley. *Artistic Approaches to Cultural Mapping: Activating Imaginaries and Means of Knowing*. Abingdon, Oxon; New York, NY: Routledge, 2018.

Duxbury, Nancy, W.F. Garrett-Petts and David MacLennan. *Cultural Mapping as Cultural Inquiry*. 1st edition. New York: Routledge, 2015.

Foster, Mike. 'The Lost Art of Critical Map Reading'. *Graphicarto* (blog). 27 February 2014. Accessed 9 April 2019. http://www.graphicarto.com/the-lost-art-of-critical-map-reading/

Givoni, Michal. 'Between Micro Mappers and Missing Maps: Digital Humanitarianism and the Politics of Material Participation in Disaster Response'. *Environment and Planning D: Society and Space* 34, no. 6 (2016): 1025–1043.

Gregory, S., M. McLagan, R. Avni, and L. Torchin. (2006). 'Technologies of Witnessing: The Visual Culture of Human Rights'. *American Anthropologist* 108, no. 1 (2006): 191–220.

Guldi, Jo. 'A History of the Participatory Map'. *Public Culture* 29, no. 1(81) (2017): 79–112. https://doi.org/10.1215/08992363-3644409

Halder, Severin and Boris Michel. 'Editorial—This Is Not an Atlas'. In *This Is Not an Atlas*, edited by kollektiv orangotango+, 14. Transcript-Verlag, 2018.

Harley, J.B. 'Deconstructing the Map'. *Cartographica* 26, no. 2 (1989): 1–20.

Harley, J.B. 'The Map and the Development of the History of Cartography'. In *The History of Cartography* 1, edited by J.B. Harley and Woodward D. Chicago: University of Chicago Press, 1987.

Huntington, S.P. 'The Clash of Civilisations?' *Foreign Affairs* 72, no. 3 (1993): 22–49.

Kitchin, Rob, Justin Gleeson and Martin Dodge. 'Unfolding Mapping Practices: A New Epistemology for Cartography'. *Transactions of the Institute of British Geographers* 38, no. 3 (2013): 480–96. https://doi.org/10.1111/j.1475-5661.2012.00540.x

Mackinder, H.J. 'The Geographical Pivot of History (1904)'. *The Geographical Journal* 170 no. 4 (1904 [2004]): 298–321.

Mapping For Rights. n.d. 'Participatory Mapping: Presenting Spatial Knowledge of Local Communities'. Accessed 23 April 2019. https://www.mappingforrights.org/participatory_mapping

Mattern, Shannon. 'Critiquing Maps'. *Words in Space* (blog), 2010. Accessed 9 April 2019. https://wordsinspace.net/shannon/2010/08/29/critiquing-maps/

Mattern, Shannon. 'Critiquing Maps II'. *Words In Space* (blog) 2013. Accessed 9 April 2019. https://wordsinspace.net/shannon/2013/09/05/critiquing-maps-ii/

Mattern, Shannon. 'Gaps in the Map: Why We're Mapping Everything, and Why Not Everything Can, or Should, Be Mapped'. *Words In Space* (blog) 2015. Accessed 16 April 2019. http://wordsinspace.net/shannon/2015/09/18/gaps-in-the-map-why-were-mapping-everything-and-why-not-everything-can-or-should-be-mapped/

Mesquita, André. 'Politics, Art and the Insurrection of Maps'. In *This Is Not an Atlas*, edited by kollektiv orangotango+, 10. Transcript-Verlag, 2018.

Norheim-Hagtun, Ida, and Patrick Meier. 'Crowdsourcing for Crisis Mapping in Haiti'. *Innovations: Technology, Governance, Globalisation* 5, no. 4 (2010): 81–89.

Obrist, Hans-Ulrich, and Tom McCarthy. *Mapping It Out: An Alternative Atlas of Contemporary Cartographies*. 1st edition. New York: Thames & Hudson, 2014.

Peluso, Nancy Lee. 'Whose Woods Are These? Counter-Mapping Forest Territories in Kalimantan, Indonesia'. *Antipode* 27, no. 4 (1995): 383–406. https://doi.org/10.1111/j.1467-8330.1995.tb00286.x

Pinder, D. 'Subverting Cartography: The Situationists and Maps of the City'. *Environment and Planning A: Economy and Space* 28 no. 3 (1996): 405–27. https://doi.org/10.1068/a280405

Polanco Masa, Alejandro. 2018. 'Google Maps Says Goodbye to Mercator (But Only on Certain Scales)'. *Maptorian* (blog), 8 August 2018. https://www.maptorian.com/google-maps-says-goodbye-to-mercator-but-only-on-certain-scales/

Schulten, S. *Mapping the Nation: History and Cartography in Nineteenth-Century America*. Chicago; London: University of Chicago Press, 2012.

Scott, James. *Seeing Like a State: How Certain Schemes to Improve the Human Condition Have Failed*. New edition. New Haven; London: Yale University Press, 1999.

Vivienne, S. and J. Burgess. 'The Remediation of the Personal Photograph and the Politics of Self-representation in Digital Storytelling'. *Journal of Material Culture* 18, no. 3 (2013): 279–298.

Wallace, A. 'Mapping City Crime and the New Aesthetic of Danger'. *Journal of Visual Culture* 8, no. 1 (2009): 5–24.

Wood, Denis and John Fels. *The Natures of Maps*. Chicago: University of Chicago Press, 2008. https://www.press.uchicago.edu/ucp/books/book/chicago/N/bo5896623.html

PART I

MAPPING CRISES

1

TRANSFORMING THE MAP?

Examining the Political and Academic Dimensions of the Environmental Justice Atlas

Lena Weber, Leah Temper and Daniela Del Bene

Introduction

Environmental justice activists, academics and activist–academics grapple daily with how to conduct politically sound theoretical work and theoretically sound political work on a topic that is both a field of study and a social movement (Temper and Del Bene 2016). The term 'environmental justice' was born in Black and Latino communities in the United States in the 1980s, as they resisted the disproportionate pollution they faced compared to white communities due to the placement of waste disposal facilities and industries. Later, it took the form of an analytical frame useful in understanding how different factors, including race, class, gender and age, shape unequal distribution of socio-environmental costs. More recently, environmental justice, both within academia and social movements, has been 'globalising', increasingly gaining in popularity and being employed as a common frame of understanding across diverse contexts, as well as a way to make visible the global dimensions of local environmental conflicts (Temper et al. 2015).

This chapter examines how political and academic goals and aspirations converge and sometimes conflict in the creation of a global-mapping project dedicated to charting this global movement for environmental justice through a database of place-based movements of environmental defence—The Environmental Justice Atlas or EJAtlas. Maps have often been used as a tool by environmental justice scholar–activists in their political and academic work (for example, the Atlas of Radical Geography[1]), though they tend to focus on individual or localised cases of environmental injustice, often in urban contexts. Like other environmental justice maps, EJAtlas was designed as an advocacy and policy tool, but with the global scope of its mapping and database, it has also become a platform for international networking and scholar–activist analysis.

Academics who are also activists, or who engage closely with social movements, have frequently discussed the often messy relationship between research and politics. From Freire's (2000) work on emancipatory praxis to rich bodies of literature by critical race theorists, feminists, queer theorists, indigenous scholars and others, scholar–activists often question how to balance the academic and political motivations and dimensions of their work (Borras 2016, Temper et al. forthcoming). Many scholar–activists might feel they have 'dual loyalties' (Hale 2006) to both their academies and a political cause or social movement. Environmental justice work, as both a movement and a body of theory (Martinez-Alier et al. 2014), must be particularly aware of these tensions, as it simultaneously takes place and develops on the streets, in the mountains, in the classroom, by our rivers. Regarding EJAtlas, its main concern is how it can be used as a tool for and by social movements, against state and corporate interests, while maintaining high academic quality.

Based on survey data from visitors to the EJAtlas website, as well as feedback received via other means, this chapter reflects on the Atlas as an example of co-produced knowledge and 'public political ecology' (Osborne 2017). It looks at who is using the Atlas and why, and at tensions and complementarities between academics and politics that arise as we attempt to map environmental conflicts for transformative goals. We, the authors, have spent years directly working with EJAtlas, and are currently one of the co-directors and founders (Leah Temper), the coordinator (Daniela Del Bene) and a doctoral candidate both studying the Atlas and assisting with its continued development (Lena Weber).

To do so, we first discuss political and academic dimensions of environmental justice work, explain the birth, growth and objectives of EJAtlas, and describe the data gathering and documentation process used by EJAtlas to map out environmental conflicts and resistance. Then, we lay out our methodology for examining how diverse actors across the globe contribute to and use the Atlas. In the resulting analysis, we examine illuminating examples of who uses the Atlas and how they use it; we also examine questions around the visuals of mapping, including accessibility and politics of representation. Finally, we discuss academic and political challenges and opportunities presented by EJAtlas, and the tensions between the two, before briefly concluding with a note on the transformative potential of the data contained in the Atlas.

But Wait, What's the Atlas?

A group of researchers at the Autonomous University of Barcelona came together in 2010 as part of a new large-scale initiative to investigate conflicts surrounding waste disposal and resource extraction in collaboration with social and environmental movements around the world. In order to systematise the information gathered about these environmental justice conflicts, the group, as part of the international EJOLT project,[2] developed an online mapping tool called the Global Atlas of Environmental Justice, or EJAtlas (Temper et al. 2015). The Atlas maps cases of local resistance to economic activities that pivot environmental impact as a key grievance via input from diverse academic and non-academic contributors from around the world (ibid.).

Grounded in theory around how power inequalities spark environmental struggles (Porto and Pacheco 2009 in Temper et al. 2015), a long history of activist-led environmental justice theory building,[3] and the need for more engaged, collaborative activist-academic knowledge production and analysis of environmental conflicts on a global scale, EJAtlas aimed to open up opportunities for political ecology[4] to move beyond case studies to a much broader, systemic analysis. The Atlas aimed to respond to critiques that environmental justice literature within academia tends to be theoretically weak and disperse (Holifield, Porter and Walker 2009 in Temper et al. 2015).

Launched once it reached a thousand cases, EJAtlas is constantly growing, with 2,600 cases mapped as of November 2018. It receives almost 2,000 unique visits daily, and has hundreds of contributors, with information on conflicts dating back as early as first the contact with colonisers. Since its launch, the Atlas has received almost three million page views by over one million users. The platform also includes featured maps, which are maps that draw attention to a particular topic or region, and that makes sense of the 'dots' on the map. Conflicts are, in fact, not stand-alone processes, but are closely tied with a whole chain of production, transportation and consumption of goods and services.

The two projects currently coordinating EJAtlas are the Environmental Justice (ENVJustice) project and Academic–Activist Co-Produced Knowledge for Environmental Justice (ACKnowl-EJ) network based at the Institute of Environmental Science and Technology in the Autonomous University of Barcelona. These projects actively add to the Atlas and seek out contributions from specific regions of the world in an effort to grow the representability of the database. In this sense, the Atlas is not an organically crowdsourced project—though, of course, organic contributions do take place—but instead, it is an invited collaborative mapping process with exact methodologies changing from region to region. An article by EJAtlas founders (Temper et al. 2015) describes in more detail the data collection methodology, but it is important to note that contributors must demonstrate a solid knowledge of the case and context. In five years, EJAtlas has engaged around 500 unique contributors from more than 100 countries.

EJAtlas uses a 'North'-oriented world map projection with conflicts depicted as small points, coloured differently depending on the overarching conflict category they correspond to. When users click on a point, a small window opens with the conflict title and the first few lines of the conflict description (see Figure 1.1). By clicking 'see more',

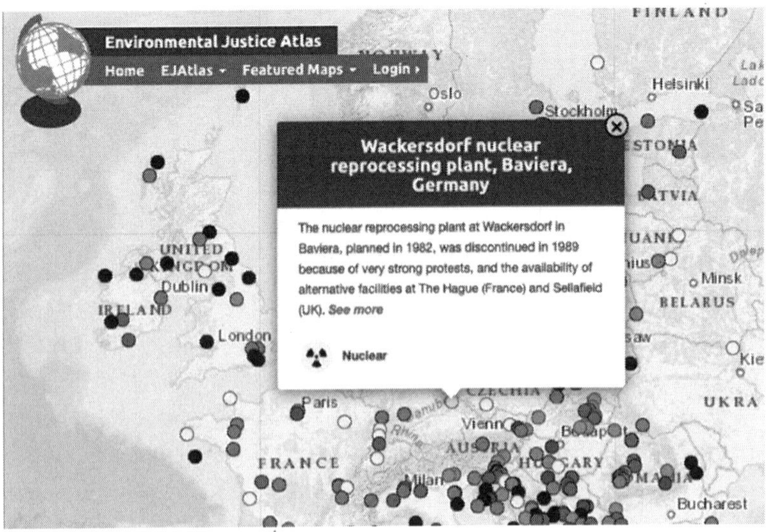

Figure 1.1: Pop-up description of individual conflict point.
Source: EJAtlas website.

the map zooms in and isolates the selected conflict, with a side panel containing images and all the information input about the case, which can be scrolled through (see Figure 1.2).

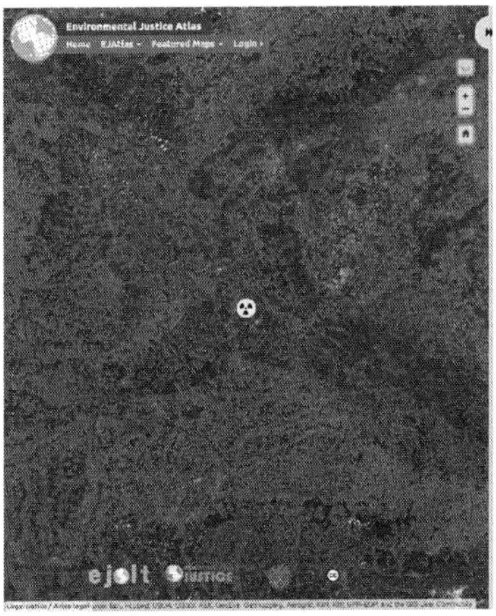

Wackersdorf nuclear reprocessing plant, Baviera, Germany

Last update:
2016-08-16

The nuclear reprocessing plant at Wackersdorf in Baviera, planned in 1982, was discontinued in 1989 because of very strong protests, and the availability of alternative facilities at The Hague (France) and Sellafield (UK).

Description:

At a cost equivalent to 5 billion euros, there were plans in the '80s to build a nuclear reprocessing plant (converting nuclear waste to nuclear fuels such as plutonium) in the Oberpfalz in Baviera, Germany. This plant was to be placed in Wackersdorf. In German, it would be a "Wiederaufbereitungsanlage", abbreviated WAA. The Anti-WAAhnsinns (Wahnsinn means "madness") were political rock concerts which took place in the 1980s, until the plans for the WAA were given up in 1989. These plans had led to major protests. German police heavily armed was confronted by demonstrators armed with slingshots, crowbars and some Molotov cocktails. The plans for the plant were abandoned due to several factors: Chernobyl, the citizens' protests, the economics of the plant, and the death of the pro-nuclear Minister-President of Bavaria Franz Josef Strauß, of the CSU (CDU), a right wing politician who was keen on building the plant. After the halt of the construction of the Wackersdorf reprocessing plant, reprocessing of spent German fuel took place in France and Britain. Once the fast breeder line was given up in Germany (because of the protests at Kalkar) there was no longer any reason for investing in large plutonium production facilities, in particular given the fact that the plants then under construction at La Hague (France) and Sellafield (UK) would have more than enough reprocessing capacity for this nasty job.

See more

Basic Data

Name of conflict:
Wackersdorf nuclear reprocessing plant, Baviera, Germany

Country:
Germany

State or province:
Schwandorf, Oberpfalz

Figure 1.2: Top: Selected conflict, Bottom: Side panel with full description of conflict point.
Source: EJAtlas website.

Featured maps go beyond conflict points to also include vector data, which can visually be turned on or off by the user, showing detailed information when clicked upon. These maps, often stemming from petitions from Environmental Justice Organisations (EJOs) or mixed academic–activist groups, also include a basic analysis of the political economy and political ecology that links together a group of conflicts and are produced with specific goals in mind (to use as a campaigning tool, for example, by an EJO). Recent examples include the Global Gas Lock-in, a map developed by activists working with London-based Gastivists and Barcelona-based Observatori del Deute en la Globalizació (ODG) to make visible resistance and conflict related to Europe's plans to grow a massive web of gas infrastructure, even while claiming to embrace policies centred on sustainability and renewables. Another example is Mujeres Tejiendo Territorio, a map developed with the Latin American Network of Women Defenders of Social and Environmental Rights and the Colombian NGO CENSAT Agua Viva—Friends of the Earth Colombia to make visible Latin American women's resistance to mining and their work in defence of life, dignity and territory. Figure 1.3 shows the clickable vector layers on a featured map called Fracking Frenzy, produced in collaboration with Friends of the Earth.

To contribute to the Atlas, visitors must create a user account and log in. Once logged in, they can generate a new conflict form to fill out. Once filled out, contributors submit the case for moderation. A member of the moderating team reviews the case and depending on the content either approves it and publishes it on the platform or writes to the contributor with suggestions for edits. The moderating team ensures that each case generally fits EJAtlas' main criteria, namely that it centres on an economic activity or legislation with negative impacts on environment and society (actual or potential), that environmental justice organisation(s) and/or local individuals claim that this harm has taken place or will likely take place and, therefore, the need to mobilise and that the conflict is documented in one or more media stories[5] (Temper et al. 2015).

Beyond mere documentation, the Atlas aims to facilitate transformative knowledge production, advocacy and activism while simultaneously contributing to ongoing theorising and networking around environmental justice issues. By making rural environmental conflicts visible, for example, it expands on the historical understanding of environmental justice struggles as primarily urban (Temper et al. 2015). Indeed, contributors to the Atlas have brought attention to more than 1,800 rural and semi-urban environmental conflicts, accounting for eighty-four per cent of all cases in the Atlas. Thus, the Atlas broadens the umbrella of environmental justice by demonstrating that issues of ecological distribution—often highlighted historically by environmental justice movements in urban United States, involving toxins and environmental racism (Pulido et al. 1996; Pulido 2000; Sicotte 2016)—are relevant in a wide diversity of socio-environmental struggles where communities claim for access to resources, health rights, land rights and more. At the same time, it addresses critiques of the overly rural and localised focus of political ecology by including hundreds of urban and semi-urban cases and globalising our understanding of environmental conflicts.

Moreover, while some goals of the Atlas are more explicitly political and others more clearly academic, there is quite a bit of overlap (Temper et al. 2015). More political goals include use of the Atlas to aid in denouncing environmental injustices, exchange of action strategies and strengthening international articulation between place-based movements, provision of reports on concrete cases and legal disputes to be used as a resource and to pressure policy-makers and politicians to support policies that are environmental justice friendly. More academic-oriented goals include theorisation, 'a statistical understanding of environmental justice struggles', and to aid 'new processes of knowledge creation' from an environmental justice perspective. Blurring the line further between the political and academic, the Atlas aims to facilitate productive lesson-learning via analysing case data, including patterns of mobilisation, success rates of resistance movements in stopping extraction projects, the impact of regulations and more (ibid.).

Finally, by mapping cases of environmental conflict on a global digital platform, EJAtlas aims to go beyond national or regional mapping,

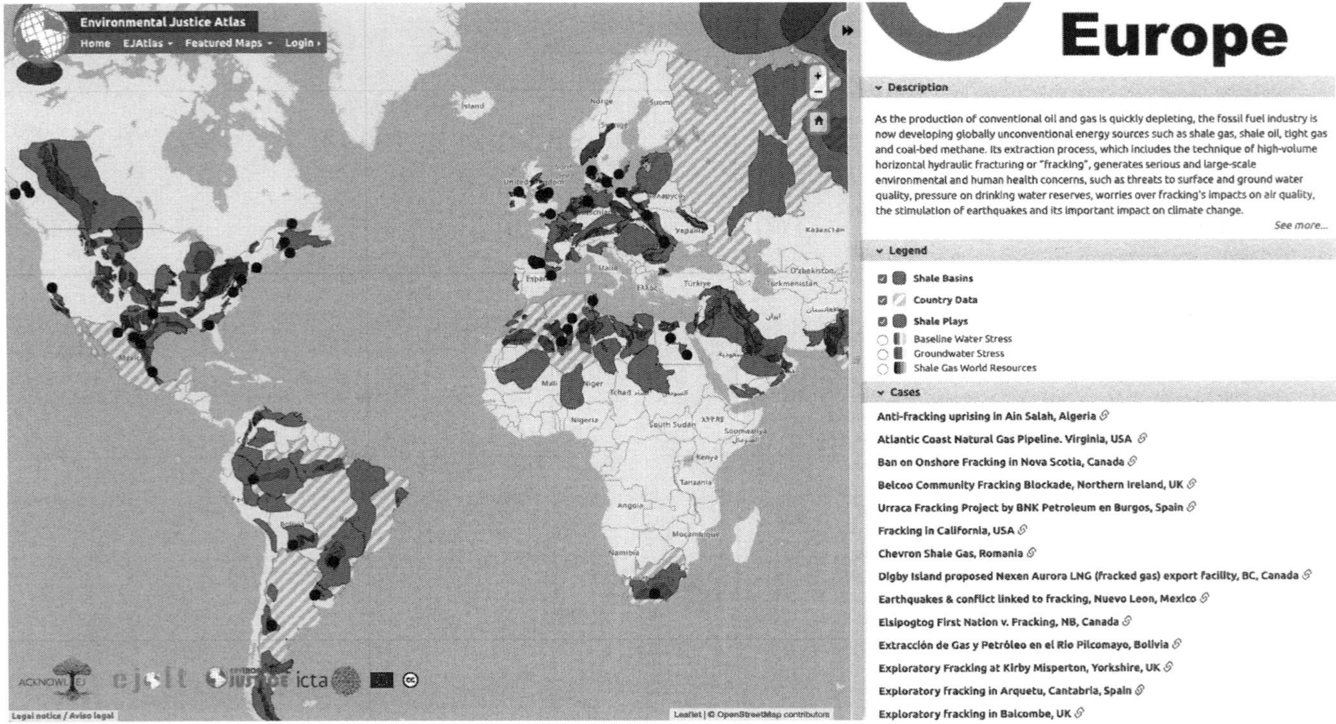

Environmental Justice Atlas
Home EJAtlas Featured Maps Login
Europe
Description
As the production of conventional oil and gas is quickly depleting, the fossil fuel industry is now developing globally unconventional energy sources such as shale gas, shale oil, tight gas and coal-bed methane. Its extraction process, which includes the technique of high-volume horizontal hydraulic fracturing or "fracking", generates serious and large-scale environmental and human health concerns, such as threats to surface and ground water quality, pressure on drinking water reserves, worries over fracking's impacts on air quality, the stimulation of earthquakes and its important impact on climate change.
See more...
Legend
Shale Basins
Country Data
Shale Plays
Baseline Water Stress
Groundwater Stress
Shale Gas World Resources
Cases
Anti-fracking uprising in Ain Salah, Algeria
Atlantic Coast Natural Gas Pipeline. Virginia, USA
Ban on Onshore Fracking in Nova Scotia, Canada
Belcoo Community Fracking Blockade, Northern Ireland, UK
Urraca Fracking Project by BNK Petroleum en Burgos, Spain
Fracking in California, USA
Chevron Shale Gas, Romania
Digby Island proposed Nexen Aurora LNG (fracked gas) export facility, BC, Canada
Earthquakes & conflict linked to fracking, Nuevo Leon, Mexico
Elsipogtog First Nation v. Fracking, NB, Canada
Extracción de Gas y Petróleo en el Rio Pilcomayo, Bolivia
Exploratory Fracking at Kirby Misperton, Yorkshire, UK
Exploratory Fracking in Arquetu, Cantabria, Spain
Exploratory Fracking in Balcombe, UK
Legal notice / Aviso legal
Leaflet | © OpenStreetMap contributors

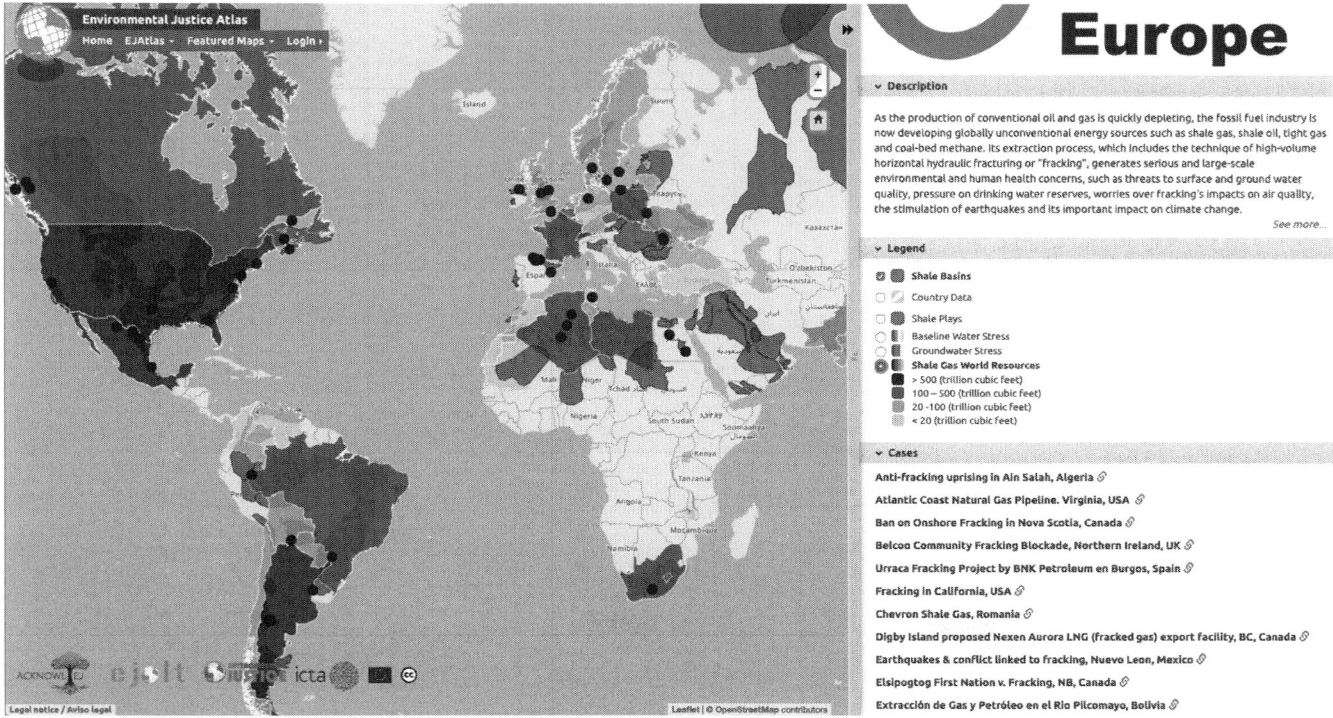

Figure 1.3: Fracky Frenzy featured map on EJAtlas with different vector layers turned on and off via the legend.

Source: EJAtlas website.

providing a tool for analysing multi-scale interactions inherent in global commodity chains, investing trends of transnational corporations, similarities across regions by type of conflicts, or groups mobilising, forms of protest and more (Del Bene et al. 2018; Avila 2018). Through this act of documentation and visibilisation, EJAtlas aims to support the transformative work of environmental justice activists and academics alike.

For this chapter, we zoom in on two key issues, as each provides important insight into the academic and political challenges and opportunities faced by such a large-scale collaborative environmental justice mapping project. These are: (a) How the Atlas is being used and contributed to, by whom, and for what? and (b) Accessibility and the politics of representation surrounding the map's writing and visuals.

To understand these issues, we primarily draw from an analysis of the EJAtlas user survey and Google Analytics, as well as direct feedback from users and contributors.

Methodology: Analysing the EJAtlas User Survey and Google Analytics

Visitors to the EJAtlas website can fill out a survey about their user profile and Atlas usage. The survey was designed to understand who is using the Atlas, for what purposes and how the tool can be improved to meet users' needs. It includes questions about user's background, where their work is based, how they rank the Atlas on a variety of factors including accessibility and recommendations for improvement, what they primarily use the Atlas for, how they define the term 'environmental justice', what elements make up a successful 'environmental justice struggle' and more. Responses from the survey were sorted in Excel sheets into multiple categories, some overlapping. Once cleaned, the full data set included 429 responses, which were sorted into six categories based on how each respondent had identified themselves, eliminating duplicate, blank and insincere responses. These six categories are Academy, Private Sector, Student, Member of Impacted Community, Government/Public Sector and Civil Society/ Environmental Justice Organisations.

Findings from the Atlas

Diverse users, diverse uses: the who, what and how of EJAtlas visitors

Beyond providing an understanding of those who use the Atlas to highlight cases, survey data reveals trends about how the Atlas is used for both—and sometimes overlapping—political (professional or otherwise) and academic (teaching and learning) goals.

Google Analytics and the EJAtlas survey reveal that the Atlas attracts users primarily from India, the United States and Colombia, in that order. This echoes the level of coverage in these countries as well as the languages the data is available in. Meanwhile, survey respondents report their work as primarily based in the United States and Colombia, followed by India and then Spain. Regionally, most respondents work in Latin America, followed by Europe, with lower representation from Africa, Canada, the United States, Asia and the Middle East.

About one-third of the respondents identified themselves as coming from civil society and/or EJOs, making individuals from this group the most frequent users of the Atlas. Students are the second most active users, followed by academics. The Atlas is used less by individuals from the government and the public sector, and communities impacted by environmental injustices, with a bit more participation from the private sector (see Figure 1.4). The relatively high representation from civil society/EJOs and low participation from members of impacted communities suggest that users of the Atlas work in an alliance, or in solidarity with affected communities, but often do not see themselves as from those communities. Though community members and civil society/EJO representatives rate the Atlas about equally regarding accessibility (in fact, community members rate it a little bit higher on average—4.1 out of 5, with 5 being the best—whereas civil society/EJO members rate it 3.9 on average), there are too few responses to conclude why so few survey respondents identify themselves as from impacted communities, if this is representative of all users and if so, why. This warrants attention and future research as the presence and participation of those directly affected by environmental injustice should be a central concern of any environmental justice project.

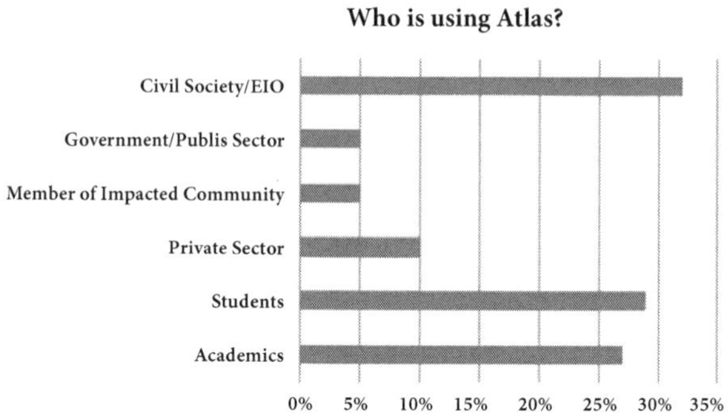

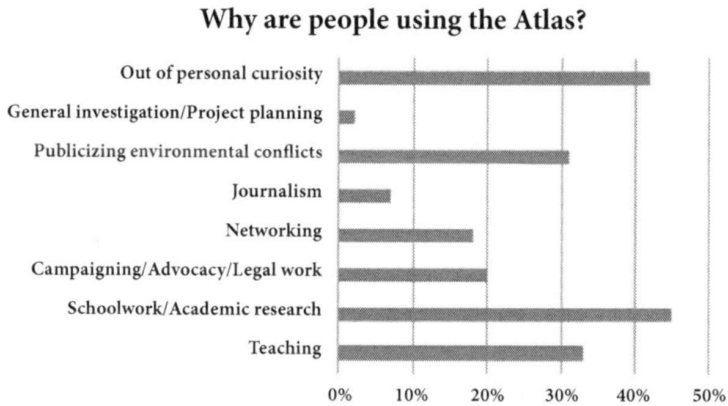

Figure 1.4: Graph showing who uses EJAtlas (left). Graph showing why people use EJAtlas (right). *Source: Authors.*

Moving on to *why* people use EJAtlas, according to survey data the Atlas' most frequent use is for schoolwork and academic research (see Figure 1.4). A closer look at the responses reveals that students from primary school[6] through doctoral programs use the Atlas for homework, school essays and dissertations; while academics frequently report using the Atlas for their research. One respondent, who is both a student and part of the private sector (working for a large international beer company), reported interest in mining and water governance and said they use the Atlas regularly for academic and personal research. A sixth-grade student from South Africa reported 'acing' her school project thanks to the Atlas information on her country, and said the Atlas is 'better than Google'.

Another frequent use of the Atlas is for teaching and presenting, in both institutional and popular settings. University professors from

Colombia, Puerto Rico and Canada use the Atlas in their classrooms as an educational tool. In South Africa and Australia, activists use the Atlas as a tool for documentation and advocacy. For example, a recent project aims to use the Atlas as a means to counteract activist burn-out and trauma. As we hear of more instances of the Atlas being used in these spaces we have focused more closely on its pedagogical potential—documenting existing uses and also actively collaborating with educators and activists to further develop teaching materials in line with the platform, and also reflect on the difficulties they have encountered in terms of accessibility, language, moderation process and more (Walter et al. forthcoming).

While schoolwork, academic research and teaching are primary uses of the Atlas by students and academics alike, including popular educational approaches by civil society and EJOs, it is interesting to examine the political use of the Atlas by other actors, such as governments and those in the public sector. Diverse uses include relying on the Atlas as a reference for public policy and planning decisions by the National Planning Agency of a Latin American country's government. A government/public administration member from a European country's federal institute of natural resources, interested in mediating and mitigating mining conflicts via implementations of development projects, reports using EJAtlas regularly for planning technical cooperation projects and writing assessment reports for their government.

Impacted communities have used the Atlas to gather information both about companies (that are behind the investments they are resisting) and networking (with other movements). For example, a member of an Australian community resisting cyanide use in mining operations at the headwaters of a water catchment wrote that through EJAtlas the community learned that the CEO of the mining company had also been CEO of a company responsible for two cyanide spills in another country because that conflict was also documented in the Atlas. They planned to take this new information to the media with the hope that it would lead to the prosecution of the CEO for providing false and misleading information. Several months later local media reported that the mining company had dropped plans to use cyanide after extensive community resistance, and the chief executive of the company resigned, though there are no reports of prosecution.

In another case, the Union de Afectados por Chevron-Texaco (UDAPT), primarily based in Ecuador, put together a small team of researchers between their office in Quito and at the EJAtlas moderation team to research other cases where the same oil company was involved. For at least three months in 2015, they reached out to communities and other EJOs involved in 30 cases, including in countries like Brazil, Australia and Kazakhstan. They published a featured map[7] on the Atlas, which showed that the impacts from the activities and bad practises of the oil giant are not sporadic, but rather systematic. The map was presented at the 2015 shareholders' assembly of Chevron in California by one of the UDAPT lawyers. At least some of the smaller investors were responsive and showed some concern. The map also had wide dissemination in national and international media and supported UDAPT's campaigning initiatives.

At the same time, we are also aware that the EJAtlas data can also be leveraged by other unscrupulous actors whose prime concern is not the pursuit of environmental justice. For example, we have been contacted by insurance companies that aim to use the EJAtlas data to set premium rates for mining companies operating internationally. While increased premiums due to knowledge about human and environmental abuses can be tentatively welcomed as a further deterrent to investment, there is concern about the potential for the data to be leveraged by international financial institutions and multinational corporations or others involved in human rights abuses. We are attentive to such concerns about misuse of the Atlas data in a way that is harmful or antithetical to the goals of environmental justice activists, as well as the risk of academic analysis that misconstrues or misunderstands the data present. In response to these concerns, we have developed mechanisms to protect contributors' privacy and offer accessibility based on shared values.

Visual representation and accessibility

This section highlights two key concerns that emerged over the first years of the Atlas: accessibility and the politics of representation. The Atlas aims to be as accessible as possible, but it is also data-heavy. When one opens the webpage they are offered an immediate snapshot of the 2,500[8] geolocated cases featured around the planet, a presentation that aims to be visually accessible but leads to potential trade-offs between visual representation and other forms of accessibility. Atlas users with less reliable or slower internet connections report glitches and failure to load, particularly on mobile devices. These same restrictions apply when inputting new cases, also due to slower internet connections in certain areas. For this reason, one potential solution currently under discussion is to develop downloadable print layouts of the maps. Another option often raised by users of the Atlas, including professors using the Atlas in their classes, has been to make the platform more mobile- and tablet-friendly. While this could increase accessibility, it remains to be seen how feasible this would be due to costs and tech support needed.

Another key issue surrounding accessibility is that English is by far the dominant language on the platform, and the case entry form is monolingual. However, there are separate language- and region-specific EJAtlas platforms for Italy and Turkey, and plans to launch an Arab regional platform entirely in Arabic soon.

Political implications of visual representation in EJAtlas

Beyond accessibility, there are other political implications of the visual aspects of the Atlas. A prime one concerns the use of a North-up Mercator projection for the map, both formats that have long been critiqued by critical cartographers and others for spatially privileging a Euro- and North America-centric view of the globe, exaggerating the physical space occupied by these regions and dramatically understating the relative size of other regions like Africa and South America. While EJAtlas is a critical mapping project and the logo itself is a South-up map, technical limitations due to the base layers available and questions of legibility mean scaffolding the data on a South-up map is not feasible.

Further, the available layers that include a topo map (the default), a world imagery map (satellite) and a landscape map present their thorny political questions regarding borders and place names included in each. Figures 1.5, 1.6 and 1.7 show the same region of the Atlas with different layers.

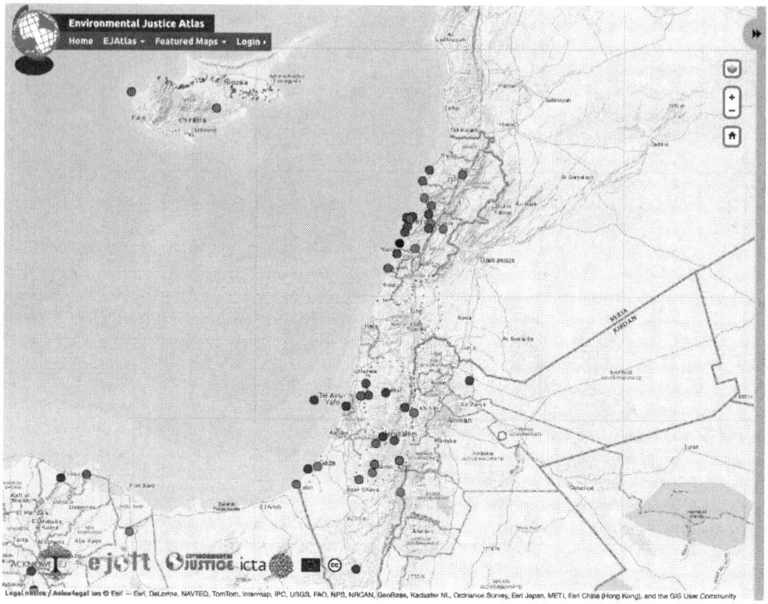

Figure 1.5: EJAtlas World Topo layer.
Source: EJAtlas website.

Figure 1.6: EJAtlas World Imagery layer.
Source: EJAtlas website.

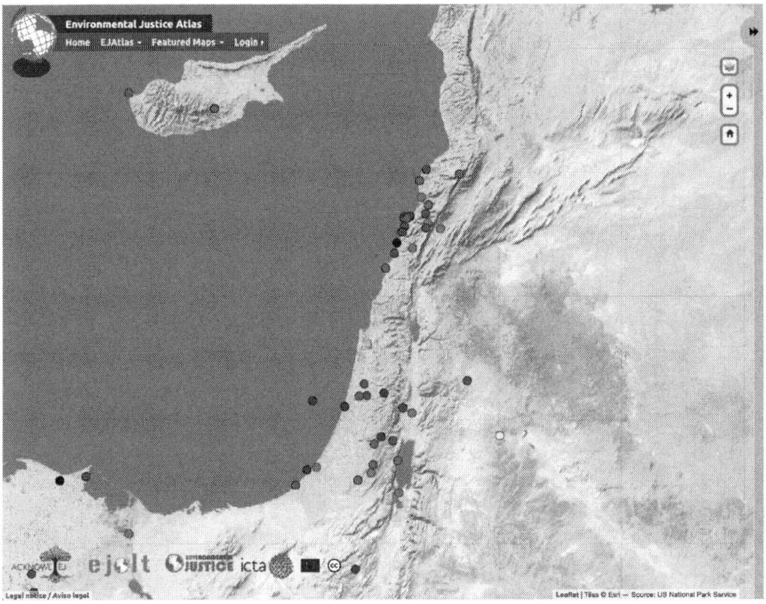

Figure 1.7: EJAtlas World Landscape layer.
Source: EJAtlas website.

As one can see, there are important differences, with political implications, between the topo and landscape layers regarding place names and borders in this region. For a project aiming to incorporate principles of sovereignty and justice, it can be contradictory to use GIS layers that divide territories, rely on colonial understandings of space and use corporate data from companies like Google.

Along these lines, the EJAtlas coordinators have been contacted by members of rights groups with concerns about colonial and corporate borders, and accompanying issues of erasure, highlighting how important and politicised representation on a digital map can be.

In reference to the depiction of Palestine on our default base map layer (the topo option), an individual wrote to the EJAtlas moderators drawing attention to issues of representation of space on one of the EJAtlas layers. They questioned the source of the original data set, saying it acted to disappear a people, its cities and its rights; and reflected an expansionist Israeli vision. In particular, they noted the lack of Arabic writing, Hebrew place names in the West Bank and East Jerusalem and incorrect lines drawn.

While this individual highlighted the political issues surrounding the depiction of borders and place names in line with global foreign power interests, another user from a Western Sahara advocacy group drew attention to the political implications of privileging a more 'local' (in this case, regional/state) power interest over global and colonial-imposed borders. They argued that the missing border demarcating Western Sahara gave the impression that the territory falls under the control of the Kingdom of Morocco, attributing this to the state of Morocco's 'powerful lobby' on the issue. They went on to provide a legal argument for why the border should be depicted—citing the history of the region, the implementation of colonial borders and international law—arguing that the border of Western Sahara implemented during colonial times is still the correct border and should appear on the Atlas.

These requests illustrate the challenges of doing an emancipatory mapping project while relying on tools such as Google Maps and ArcGIS. As a response to these comments we sought alternative base maps, but there were none available that fit our needs. If resources permit, we hope to create a topographical layer that does so in future.

Discussion and Conclusion

In this chapter, we briefly explored some political and academic dimensions of the Environmental Justice Atlas (EJAtlas). Several years' worth of survey data from the Atlas users along with direct feedback and Google Analytics provides insight into (a) how the Atlas is being used and contributed to, by whom and for what and (b) accessibility and the politics of representation surrounding the map's writing and visuals, helping guide the project forward in order to meet its transformative goals.

This type of collaborative activist–academic projects can be considered 'co-production of knowledge', as a way to recognise that the knowledge produced and/or made visible through them comes as a result of engaged interactions not isolated to either just the university or just a social movement or organisation. Survey data from EJAtlas supports an understanding of the Atlas data as 'co-produced', due to the diversity of the individuals contributing and analysing cases, and also highlights how different actors involved in such a collaborative process may be approaching it with very different motivations, needs and perspectives.

In co-production processes, one might expect that this would happen; that each actor would approach the project with their own understandings and conceptualisations. However, often, co-production processes take place on a smaller scale between groups that share contexts and perhaps more common goals. EJAtlas provides an interesting case to examine what happens in co-production processes that transcend the local, with co-producers situated in very distinct and diverse contexts around the world. Future work will delve deeper into this aspect of the Atlas, including an analysis of the hundreds of survey responses defining 'environmental justice' and 'environmental justice success'.

Arizona-based political ecologist Tracey Osborne (2017) calls EJAtlas an example of public political ecology (PPE), which she offers as a form of engaged scholarship in the context of an ecological crisis that incorporates political, ethical and educational aspects. Drawing on Antonio Gramsci's idea of the philosophy of praxis, PPE sees ideas as a material with revolutionary transformative potential, and mapping as one important methodological approach for political ecologists to engage with the broader public in a potentially emancipatory way.

Indeed, survey results support her analysis, at least of the incorporation of the political, ethical and educational aspects, and the transformative potential of the co-produced knowledge present in the Atlas, with a possible concrete example found in the resignation of a CEO and moratorium on arsenic use in a mining case. However, the results also highlight the complications and opportunities of a 'public political ecology' project that engages with and is shaped by such a large and diverse 'public'.

In particular, this project highlights the frequent trade-offs one must often make between different priorities and aspects of work that is both academic and politicised. One clear example of this emerges around the issue explored—of accessibility and 'just' representation, which may change depending on the context of each user and what may be most 'politically correct' from their perspective (which may or may not collide with other users' perspectives). Efforts to alter the visuals of the map to more justly represent various spaces would likely impact the accessibility of the map, perhaps in both positive and negative ways and vice versa.

Further ethical questions of a political nature emerge around the potential use of the Atlas data by the private sector and governments in a repressive way, and concerns about how corporations, insurance companies and others might use the data for exploitative or for-profit activities. We must be acutely aware of the possible issues of accessibility and lack of engagement of those on the frontlines of environmental injustices, and how to incorporate feedback regarding the design and visual representation when considering issues of justice—balancing, for example, the already mentioned issue surrounding ease of diffusion and widespread accessibility (including the need to not overload the server with too complex of a database) with multiple language needs and diverse political understandings of borders and place names.

Challenges of an academic nature are also found in this type of project, though many have a political trade-off. For example, there are complications for analysis of data collected via different methodological approaches depending on the region, yet this arguably makes the project more attentive to the heterogeneity of regional needs and design priorities (for example, the development of regional platforms managed and designed by activists and academics from those same regions). On the other hand, many academics request access to the full data set in excel format, which would aid them in their processes of academic analysis. Yet, thus far we have denied this access to the vast majority due to the lack of a data use guideline policy, and concerns about the misuse and misinterpretation of the data, along with some security concerns, all of which could endanger the transformative political work of the Atlas contributors. The current framework for allowing access to the full data set also privileges early-career environmental justice scholar–activists with job precarity closest to the project and contributing the most to the data set, over less involved, later-career researchers, thereby, at least partially, attempting to dissuade cases of academic extractivism.

EJAtlas has a long future ahead, and we are excited to continue to explore its potential, tackling complex political and academic challenges as they arise. While mapping these conflicts in a just way presents difficulties, feedback and engagement from the ever-growing group of users and contributors from around the world help us hone the Atlas to act not just as a documentation platform, but as a tool that can work to *transform* the very conflicts and patterns it depicts.

Notes

1. http://www.an-atlas.com/
2. EJOLT or Environmental Justice Organisations, Liabilities and Trade, began in 2012 with 'Science in Society' funds from the European FP7 programme, and had 23 academic institutions and activist group partners from around the world.
3. For example, key concepts born from grassroots movements include environmental racism, food sovereignty, environmentalism of the poor, biopiracy, green deserts, ecocide and more (Martinez-Alier et al. 2014).
4. Political ecology politicises environmental issues by examining the political, social and economic factors impacting the environment and human/society-environment interactions. A relatively young field, it aims to offer an alternative to apolitical ecology and environmental studies (EJOLT 2013). http://www.ejolt.org/2013/02/political-ecology/
5. While not all cases in the Atlas fit this criteria perfectly, most do. At times, because of the rural-ness of a case or media repression, a case might not appear in many media stories, but if there are other reliable sources of information it can still be included in the Atlas.
6. The youngest student identified in the survey is a 6th grade student from South Africa.
7. The map is accessible at this link: http://ejatlas.org/featured/chevronconflicts
8. As of October 2018.

References

Avila S. 'Environmental Justice and the Expanding Geography of Wind Power Conflicts'. *Sustainability Science* 13, no. 3 (2018): 599–616.

Borras, S.M. 'Land Politics, Agrarian Movements, and Scholar–Activism' (Paper presented at the International Institute of Social Studies, Erasmus University, 14 April 2016). http://repub.eur.nl/pub/93021/Jun_Borras_Inaugural_14Apr2016.pdf (accessed 8 February 2017).

Del Bene D., A. Scheidel and L. Temper. 'More Dams, More Violence? A Global Analysis on Resistances and Repression Around Conflictive Dams Through Co-Produced Knowledge'. *Sustainability Science* 13, no. 3 (2018): 617–633.

Freire, P. Pedagogy of the Oppressed. Chicago: Bloomsbury Publishing, 2000.

Hale, C.R. 'Activist Research v. Cultural Critique: Indigenous Land Rights and the Contradictions of Politically Engaged Anthropology'. *Cultural Anthropology* 21, no. 1 (2006): 96–120.

Martinez-Alier J., I. Anguelovski, P. Bond, D. Del Bene, F. Demaria, J.-F. Gerber, L. Greyl, W. Haas, H. Healy, V. Marín-Burgos, G. Ojo, M. Porto, L. Rijnhout, B. Rodríguez-Labajos, J. Spangenberg, L. Temper, R. Warlenius and I. Yanez.

'Between Activism and Science: Grassroots Concepts for Sustainability Coined by Environmental Justice Organisations'. *Journal of Political Ecology* 21, no. 1 (2014): 19–60.

Osborne, T. 'Public Political Ecology: A Community of Praxis for Earth Stewardship'. *Journal of Political Ecology* 24, no. 1 (2017): 843–860.

Pulido, L. 'Rethinking Environmental Racism: White Privilege and Urban Development in Southern California'. *Annals of the Association of American Geographers* 90, no. 1 (2000): 12–40.

Pulido, L., S. Sidawi and R.O. Vos. 'An Archaeology of Environmental Racism in Los Angeles'. Urban Geography 17, no. 1 (1996): 419–439. DOI: 10.2747/0272-3638.17.5.419

Sicotte, D. 'The Importance of Historical Methods for Building Theories of Urban Environmental Inequality'. *Environmental Sociology* 2, no. 3 (2016): 254–264.

Temper, L. and D. Del Bene. 'Transforming Knowledge Creation for Environmental and Epistemic Justice'. *Current Opinion in Environmental Sustainability* 20 (2016): 41–49. DOI: 10.1016/j.cosust.2016.05.004

Temper, L., D. Del Bene and J. Martinez-Alier. 'Mapping the Frontiers and Frontlines of Global Environmental Justice: the EJAtlas'. *Journal of Political Ecology* 22, no. 1 (2015): 255–278.

Temper, L., D. McGarry and L. Weber. 'The Tarot Deck of Transgressive Research: A Reflexive Device for Political Rigour'. *Ecological Economics* 64 (2019); 106379.

Walter, M., L. Weber and L. Temper. 'Learning and Teaching Through the Online Environmental Justice Atlas: From Empowering Activists to Motivating Students'. New Directions for Teaching and Learning (forthcoming).

2

HUMANITARIAN TRACKER

Crowdsourcing and Artificial Intelligence for Social Good

Hend Alhinnawi and Taha Kass-Hout

As the cold wind roared on a dark, snowy November night in 2016, more than 150 people, mostly women and children, were trapped in Eastern Aleppo, Syria. They were trying to escape bombs falling from the sky and shelling around them, but could not seem to find a safe evacuation route. Time was running out and so was their hope for survival. Meanwhile, 5,000 miles away, in Washington, DC, Humanitarian Tracker's team was contacted by Steven Livingston, a visiting Harvard professor who was coordinating with a small, informal coalition, to help get the trapped families out. He asked if there was any data about safe evacuation routes. Our team quickly sifted through reports we had received from Aleppo and tried to contact people on the ground. In the meantime, experts were monitoring live satellite imagery coming in from Aleppo, to figure out a safe way out. Hours went by and the situation became increasingly grim.

After looking at various reports received by Syria Tacker—the flagship project of Humanitarian Tracker—from the ground and speaking with trusted sources, our team came to the one conclusion that made sense. For their own safety, these 150 people needed to stay exactly where they were because at that time there was no safe evacuation route available. Our reports at Humanitarian Tracker confirmed what the group concerned with saving the people on the ground had suspected when looking at the live satellite imagery (Livingston and Drake 2017). Technology and innovation are good tools that can be applied to the humanitarian space in many ways, but at the end of the day, they are only tools. True power comes when people are put in the centre of, and at the intersection of all decisions made. Whether you are in Aleppo in Syria or Los Angeles in California, citizen engagement aided by technology can transcend borders and conflict to save lives.

People Power

Humanitarian Tracker was founded in 2012 to connect and empower citizens by using innovation in technology for humanitarian events around the world and to elevate otherwise marginalised voices. It was founded by Hend Alhinnawi, international development and public diplomacy professional, and Taha Kass-Hout, a cardiologist and a leader in health care and artificial intelligence. Over the years, we have seen first-hand how people defy odds to share their stories, strengthen their communities and strive to create a more inclusive environment for all. Technological innovations today shape the way that people respond to humanitarian crises. From the early stages of disasters to relief and recovery efforts, our experiences tell us that engaging with communities online during and after crises and disasters is fundamental. The people on the ground are usually the best sources of information for what has happened, when it happened and what the current situation may look like. They will tell you, perhaps better than any expert assessment, what is needed. They are key to providing the world with critical information, such as updates on breakouts of violence and war, disease epidemics or natural disasters while helping to coordinate relief efforts to those most in need.

Our mission at Humanitarian Tracker is to empower citizens and bring their voices to the decision-making table. This involves prioritising the needs and perspectives of people who are at the centre of disasters, conflicts, or relief and development needs. We believe that this is particularly vital, not only during crises but also in achieving long-term global goals, including the UN Sustainable Development Goals (which we will address later in the chapter). By providing a platform for these communities to share information, we hope to enhance their ability to mobilise resources, humanitarian relief and organise community-based outreach along with international organisations.

Humanitarian Tracker combines crowdsourcing (which engage large groups of people to perform tasks such as collecting data) with data mining and machine learning techniques to provide the best possible, timely and accurate information for those working in disaster response, relief and development within humanitarian events or crises.

Using these methods, our team works globally to document human rights violations, casualties, relief efforts and humanitarian needs. As a 501(c)(3) non-profit, non-partisan effort, we are strictly dedicated to supporting humanitarian causes. In doing so, we believe that innovation is not always the next shiny new thing. In fact, sometimes, being innovative means taking existing technology, platform, or tool and repurposing it for a specific need. In our case, we have used techniques that were successfully tried in disease detection, with proven precision and accuracy (Kass-Hout and Zhang 2010; Goth 2013).

In this chapter, we explore one of our main projects, Syria Tracker,[1] as it has been referenced as the longest-standing crowdsourced effort to date. Together, we will walk through how our team applied technology to empower citizens that would have otherwise been forgotten, ultimately representing a great example of ordinary people doing extraordinary things (Red Cross Red Crescent 2014).

Case Study: Syria Tracker

In 2011, when the conflict broke out in Syria, there was little information coming from the ground and people had no idea what was happening (Humanitarian Tracker 2011). We developed Syria Tracker, the flagship project of Humanitarian Tracker, in 2011, a few weeks into the conflict, with the intention to give citizens on the ground a chance to tell the world what was happening to and around them. It was started because a small group of concerned citizens in the United States wanted to understand what was happening on the ground, and felt that by giving a voice to ordinary citizens, they could then begin to understand and piece together the situation. Syria Tracker was created as an online platform, where people on the ground could submit reports accompanied by pictures, videos and information from the ground. The reports received by Syria Tracker were submitted by men and women from various age groups, and they covered a multitude of topics ranging from human rights violations to disease outbreaks and humanitarian needs. It was also spread out across Syria and represented many sides of the conflict. After reports began to come into Syria Tracker, people in Syria began using the reports to understand what was happening in other parts of the country and look for loved ones who were missing, while the rest of the world, including government agencies, UN organisations, media outlets along with others searched for clues on what was happening inside the country.

Syria Tracker's ultimate goal is not to provide numbers, but to preserve the name and location of each victim in this unfolding tragedy, so that they will not have died in vain, and to derive overall insights that can drive data-driven policy and advocacy (Jewell et al. 2018). Whenever possible, each death is also linked with photo and video evidence that, although it may be graphic and disturbing, does support the recommendations of the UN Human Rights Council and the International Criminal Court to create a documented record so that crimes against civilians will not be forgotten (Sarfaty 2017; Hubrecht 2017; Alston and Knuckey 2016; Shiel 2013).

Sources and Method

During a disaster or crisis, the most crucial information is often missing, and responders are unable to reach those most affected. When the conflict started in Syria, there was very little information coming out of official news sources. Some of the most powerful images and stories came from eyewitness reports on the ground. That was made possible by providing a platform like Syria Tracker, so people could have the power to report what is happening to and around them. The Syria Tracker platform has allowed for people on the ground in Syria and elsewhere to tell their own stories. Using a simple technology—a cell phone—one can take a picture or video and upload it on the website or Twitter. It gives power and a voice to the people, so the world can hear. The beauty of this platform is that it can be scaled and used in other regions around the world, and for all types of disasters and crises. Syria Tracker provides:

1. a continually updated list of eye witness reports from within Syria, often accompanied by media links,
2. aggregated reports including analysis and visualisations of deaths and atrocities, epidemics, relief needs, human right violations, etc. in Syria and neighbouring countries and
3. a stream of content, filtered and curated media from news, social media (Twitter and Facebook) and official sources.

The Syria Tracker platform allows people on the ground, including victims, to submit reports about what is happening to them and around them to one place. For example, in Syria, citizens were able to document atrocities such as killings and rapes, as well as disease outbreaks, relief and refugee needs, etc. The information received by Syria Tracker is verified and published publicly, allowing entities around the world, including the United Nations, USAID and US Department of State, among others, to use the data to lead policy discussions and relief, and to gain a more complete picture of the situation in Syria. Communities within Syria have used Syria Tracker to connect with relief efforts and learn about incidents in their neighbouring jurisdiction. Our goal is to apply the same methods and techniques used in the Syria conflict to other events and disasters.

Syria Tracker receives reports from people on the ground through several sources, including e-mail, the Syria Tracker website, or the Syria Tracker twitter handle (@syriatracker). The reports are often accompanied by supporting pictures or videos. Our team also organises otherwise unstructured information from YouTube videos and reports by non-governmental organisations. The platform also mines data from other sources from the web, including official news reports, social media (Twitter and Facebook) and blogs, for reports about human rights violations in Syria. The website was developed to leverage information that is produced by citizen reporters, in collaboration with a variety of other entities, and made publicly available to produce a free centralised source of information. Based on our monitoring of the Syrian conflict, we understand that events unfold over time, and new complementary (or sometimes conflicting) reports keep arriving from different sources, including ordinary citizens, government entities, NGOs and refugees.[2] Bringing together these different sources of data, Syria Tracker offers a crisis mapping system that uses crowdsourced text, photo and video reports to form a live map of the events in Syria. Since it was launched in April 2011, Syria Tracker has received more than 200,000 geotagged eye witness reports from citizen journalists and has collected over one million official news reports and close to one billion social media posts, creating a living record of the progression of the conflict and its aftermath.

A critical outcome of the reports submitted by citizens is the ability to shed light on otherwise unreported issues. These include, for example, the first case of polio that re-emerged in Syria; reports on the 'death routes', including tracking of drownings and exhaustion-related deaths in the Mediterranean Sea; as well as the increasing proportion of females being killed in Syria due to the targeting of civilians.[3] Syria Tracker illustrates the important role of crowdsourcing, network data analysis, machine learning for accurately analysing large and complex volume of data and data visualisation in human rights documentation and beyond (Rall et al. 2016; Dardagan and Salama 2013).

Privacy, ethics and security

Our team at Humanitarian Tracker is invested in protecting citizens' security and privacy and has put mechanisms into place to do so. Humanitarian Tracker offers tools for crowdsourcing intelligence that addresses the two biggest concerns of citizen journalism, especially in a war zone: protecting the identities of its reporters and ensuring the accuracy of its reports. There are several ways that allow secure and anonymous submission of reports, while also providing tips to citizens on how to protect their identities. For example, we produced a short video instructing people on ways to protect themselves and their identities when they submit reports, such as by creating temporary e-mail IDs that automatically expire in ten minutes (Gutiérrez 2018). Based on these methods, we helped develop with Oxford University 'Every Casualty Standards' for casualty recording (Standards for Casualty Recording 2016).

Impact and implications

Syria Tracker ensures timely response to crises and disasters by creating a sustainable and efficient model for users. A prompt response can be initiated by knowing which areas are in need of resources and immediate medical aid. Syria Tracker helps coordinate relief efforts through information sharing and needs assessment. Sharing information on a public platform has helped agencies understand what is most needed, and leverage their resources to combine efforts and increase efficiency (Gjøsæter and Radianti 2018; Tomaszewski 2014; Rogstadius 2015; Finch et al. 2016).

Since its launch, Syria Tracker has become the longest standing crowdsourced project to date (Ushahidi 2015) and all through one of the most austere conditions in human history. By empowering people on the ground, Syria Tracker was able to capture a steady stream of inputs that are crowdsourced from people caught in the Syria crisis, and from over 2,000 news sources and online content (Twitter, Facebook, YouTube, etc.). The information is displayed on a digital map with layers of events tagged with metadata, auto-generated using machine learning and curated for active learning and accuracy, and arrayed geospatially and chronologically. Quality control and human curation are essential. Only 6 per cent of the 200,000 crowdsourced reports to date have been published. This low percentage highlights strict standards for determining the validity in precision and accuracy of information received by Syria Tracker. The reports cover killings, missing people, rapes, use of chemical weapons, disease outbreaks and refugees and their needs. Our team helped uncover and report on forty-seven massacres targeting civilians not recorded by the media or other humanitarian organisations.

Our experience with Syria Tracker has shown that crowdsourcing combined with machine learning and human curation along with automated mining of a massive mainstream of information can provide a unique opportunity for event detection, maintaining situation awareness and enabling timely and effective policy decisions and response (Kass-Hout and Alhinnawi 2013). Syria Tracker has been collecting information from citizens, social media and news reports, allowing citizens, governments, international agencies and those that create and execute policy decisions to use this information and share it.

In applying crowdsourcing with data mining and machine learning techniques, Syria Tracker has already highlighted the potential impact of these tools and technologies. For example, Save the Children claimed its 2014 polio vaccination campaign in northern Syria vaccinated everyone. However, after Syria Tracker analysed the data received from a partner agency on the ground, it was discovered that approximately 23,000 children were not given the vaccine. Syria Tracker's analysis led Save the Children to return to the region and vaccinate all those that they had missed the first time around. This would almost certainly never have happened had the data not been open and publicly available. Transparency was thus crucial. This story highlights the critical link between human rights, accountability, optics and data sharing. Thus, while Syria Tracker cannot specify how many people have died, it can help uncover trends and insights that can inform policy and humanitarian interventions.

The platform is able to address current scalability challenges during crises, mass disasters, or conflicts, for tracking the events as they unfold and is unique in how it automats data mining, event classification and detection using machine learning, and curation processes, in addition to a simplified visualisation component for better usability and access. Building on our specific experience with Syria, and our deep understanding of the current landscape of available solutions and their limitations, Humanitarian Tracker has built a platform to assure scalability and stability, and to add new features that emerged from the work in Syria with citizens on the ground and international aid organisations.

Findings

Working with our partners, including SumAll and Ushahidi, the Humanitarian Tracker team analysed trends and patterns such as civilian targeting and the rising proportion of female deaths over the course of the conflict (see Figures 2.1, 2.2 and 2.3). One proxy to understanding civilian targeting is unarmed women, and according to Syria Tracker's data, 85 per cent of those casualties result from artillery (large calibre guns, shelling, tanks, etc.), gunshots or air bombardment. These types of casualties are consistent with collateral damage—women could simply be bystanders. The proportion of female deaths in Syria, however, has continued to increase steadily from less than 1 per cent in April 2011 to over 18 per cent today, suggesting civilian targeting. Other top causes of female deaths, such as sniper fire, beating and stabbing are typically associated with deliberate, targeted killings. We have found that sniper fire is used systematically across Syria in an indiscriminate fashion towards men, women and children. Female victims were also part of many massacres—including the spike of killings in 2015—with the highest ever number of 79 victims of targeted female deaths on a single day on 25 June 2015 in a single *nahya* (sub-district) in Kobanî (`Ayn al-`Arab) since the conflict started in Syria.

Children continue to be one of the primary targets in Syria. To date, approximately 11.5 per cent of all documented killings by Syria Tracker are children. More than 75 per cent of children were killed by explosive weapons, including artillery, missiles, or air bombardment, with at least 5 per cent of children killing being targeted. For example, during the first two years of the conflict (March 2011 to November 2014), Syria Tracker has documented approximately 14,000 confirmed killings of children under the age of eighteen obtained from crowdsourced reports. Over 755 children were executed by beating, stabbing, burning, torture, or sniper, including more than 300 babies (under two) killed by small arms. Over 500 children died from sniper attacks.

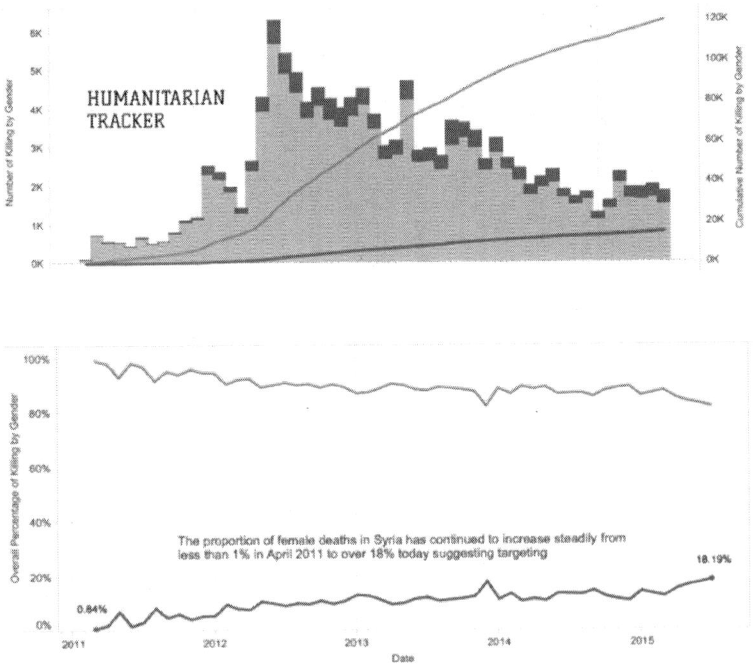

Figure 2.1: Data analytics on female deaths in Syria.
Source: Humanitarian Tracker website.

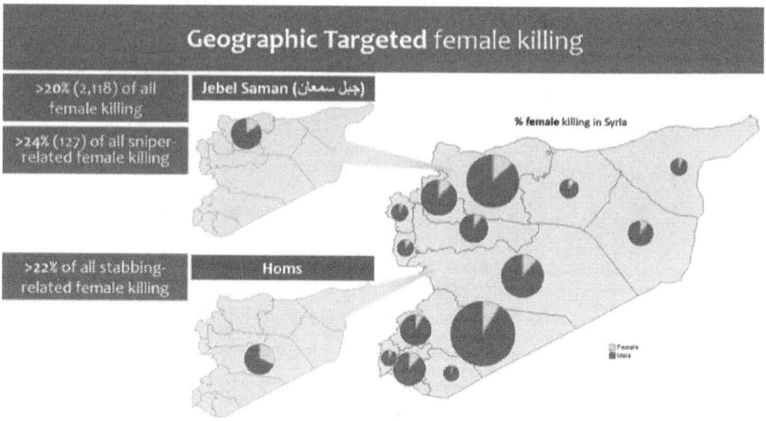

Figure 2.2: Geographic concentrations of targeted female killings.
Source: Humanitarian Tracker website.

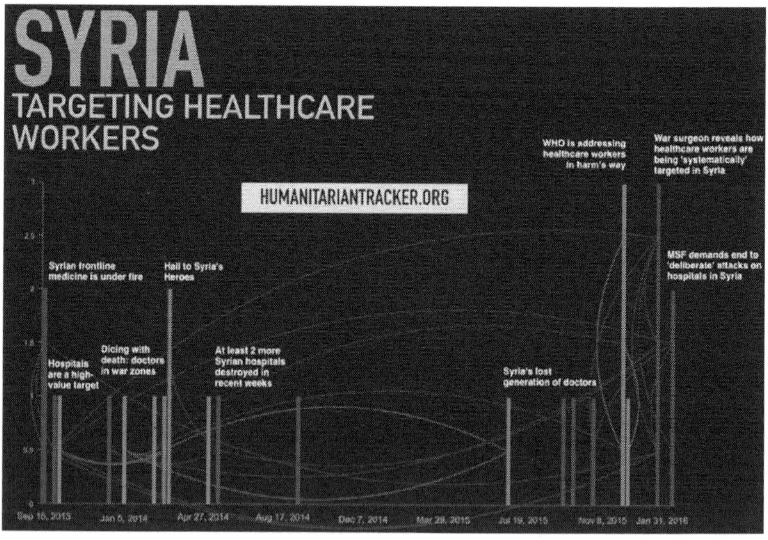

Figure 2.3: Data analytics on the targeting of healthcare workers.
Source: Humanitarian Tracker website.

Reflecting on these findings we have continued to develop and evolve the platform to ensure a timely response to these crises and disasters. Creating a more sustainable and efficient model for users—particularly through information provided by victims on the ground—means knowing what areas are most in need of resources and medical aid. We thus work to coordinate relief efforts through information sharing and needs assessment by helping agencies understand what is most needed, and leverage their resources to combine efforts and increase efficiency.

A single place to pull together disparate reports on human rights violations in a crowdsourced way is crucial to make sense of the broader pattern of abuse and to demonstrate a widespread and systematic attack on civilians, the legal qualification of crimes against humanity. Syria Tracker, one of the main projects of Humanitarian Tracker, documented and mapped a large body of verified evidence mostly generated directly by citizens affected by the conflict. We hope these documentations serve as evidence on where harm was inflicted upon citizens in Syria. This is important in order to change the nature of advocacy around the plight of not only the people in Syria but others around the world.

What's Next?

With 75 per cent of the world's population carrying mobile phones, individuals increasingly have the technological means to document and publicise their status. This rise in adoption of mobile phones and the Internet,[4] in both industrialised and developing countries, has provided additional opportunities in crowdsourcing. Mobile phones are particularly important because they function in remote locations and are readily carried and used at any time. Additionally, because smartphone applications include the capability to register GPS coordinates, verification of the proximity of citizen reporters to their locations can also be used as a validation and verification tool. Enhanced access to the Internet over the past few years indicates that the world can hear about and respond to reports of events taking place, even inside repressive regimes. This activity and reactivity may occur in near real-time, allowing individuals around the world to access volumes of data made easily digestible to diverse audiences through live maps and other visualisation techniques.

Crowdsourcing efforts around the world have been able to track events or relief needed—such as tracking oil spills, election intimidation, corruption, tornados, power outages, civil wars and food and water requests after an earthquake etc.—from multiple channels, including e-mail, Twitter, YouTube videos, online news, syndicated feeds (such as Really Simple Syndication or RSS), webform and mobile apps, among others. In the case of Syria, citizens used Syria Tracker to document atrocities (killing, rape, disease outbreaks, relief and refugee needs, etc.). Since its establishment in 2011, Syria Tracker has been described as one of the most reliable sources on what is happening on the ground. And we are not stopping there.

In 2016, Humanitarian Tracker was recognised as a top global innovation that could be applied to the Sustainable Development Goals and was showcased at the Solutions Summit hosted at the United Nations. Building on that momentum, we are embarking on a journey to crowdsource the United Nations' Global Goals, set to be achieved by 2030.[5] The Sustainable Development Goals are a universal call to action. They represent seventeen ambitious targets including ending poverty, gender equality, climate change, peace and justice, innovation and sustainable consumption, to name a few. As our world is interconnected, so are these goals. In order to achieve Global Goals, citizens around the world need to be part of the process. There is a tremendous movement of global citizens working on various goals, and Humanitarian Tracker aims to crowdsource what ordinary people are doing in their respective communities to achieve the UN Global Goals through our new project, the Global Action Mosaic.

The Global Action Mosaic, in partnership with the United Nations Foundation, is an all-inclusive project that aims to collect data around the Global Goal, meaning anyone from a farmer working in the fields of Pakistan using clean energy to governments creating more gender-equal systems are invited to be part of the mosaic. Ultimately, the goals of the Global Action Mosaic are simple. It aims to harness and showcase the power of ordinary people doing extraordinary things, through crowdsourcing projects globally around the Sustainable Development Goals (SDGs). It also aims to be part of the effort to track and measure progress made towards SDGs globally, and to raise awareness about SDGs to improve the chances of achieving them. Launched in September 2018, we plan to present this live-action mosaic annually during the Global Goals Week in September, from now and adding progress until 2030.

Disasters, epidemics and wars will continue to happen, and as innovations in technology continue to advance, so should the way we collect information, coordinate timely response and help those most in need. While there is no silver bullet solution, we hope that our experience at Humanitarian Tracker can provide a roadmap to addressing large scale disasters and conflicts. In addition to the use of technology, a model of information sharing between organisations should be adopted and promoted. In the end, we are all in this together, and one of the ways we can mobilise and respond efficiently is through making information available to all stakeholders.

Appendix 1: Actionable Information

- Steven Livingston and Jonathan Drake, 'We Tried to Save 150 People in Aleppo from 5,000 Miles Away', *The Washington Post*, 9 January 2017. The Carr Center for Human Rights Policy, Harvard Humanitarian Initiative and American Association for the Advancement of Science (AAAS) together corroborated evidence using near-real-time satellite imagery and reported from the ground on Syria Tracker. https://www.washingtonpost.com/news/monkey-cage/wp/2017/01/09/we-tried-to-save-150-people-in-aleppo-from-5000-miles-away/?noredirect=on&utm_term=.98627d61a163
- B. Tajaldin, K. Almilaji, P. Langton and A. Sparrow, 'Defining Polio: Closing the Gap in Global Surveillance', *Annals of Global Health* 81, no. 3 (June 2015): 386–395. https://www.annalsofglobalhealth.org/articles/abstract/10.1016/j.aogh.2015.06.007/
- Sophie Cousins, 'Syria Struggles to Vaccinate Residents', *Aljazeera*, 23 November 2014. https://www.aljazeera.com/news/middleeast/2014/11/syria-struggles-vaccinate-residents-201411237180769415.html
- USAID USG Humanitarian Assistance Syria—Complex Emergency. Sample map available at: https://www.usaid.gov/sites/default/files/documents/1866/Syria%20Complex%20Emergency%20Program%20Map.pdf
- Syrian Refugee Crisis Map, *The Washington Post*, 17 December 2013. Syria Tracker is one of the data sources used to create this map. https://www.washingtonpost.com/world/syrian-refugee-crisis-map/2013/12/13/f45b570e-645b-11e3-a373-0f9f2d1c2b61_graphic.html?utm_term=.730338188f9d

Appendix 2: Insights

- Irene Pavesi, 'Tracking Conflict-related Deaths: A Preliminary Overview of Monitoring Systems', Small Arms Survey, February 2017. http://www.smallarmssurvey.org/fileadmin/docs/M-files/Armed_violence/SAS-Monitoring-conflict-deaths.pdf
- Mireille Widmer and Irene Pavesi, 'Firearms and Violent Deaths', *Small Arms Survey Research Note 60*, October 2016. http://www.smallarmssurvey.org/fileadmin/docs/H-Research_Notes/SAS-Research-Note-60.pdf
- David Kilcullen and Nate Rosenblatt, 'The Rise of Syria's Urban Poor', 18 April 2014. http://cco.ndu.edu/Portals/96/Documents/prism/prism_4-syria/The_Rise_Of_Syrias_Urban_Poor.pdf
- Following the Headstamp Trail, 15 April 2014. This report examines the headstamps of seventy different types of small calibre ammunition, and analyses images of cartridge types, packaging and contextual information such as weapons systems and combatants. Syria Tracker was one of the open-source data used in this report. http://www.smallarmssurvey.org/fileadmin/docs/F-Working-papers/SAS-WP18-Syria-Headstamp-Trail.pdf
- Nicolas Florquin, 'Arms Prices and Conflict Onset: Insights from Lebanon and Syria', *European Journal on Criminal Policy and Research* 20, no. 3 (3 May 2014): 323–341. The strong correlations observed in the article suggest that crowdsourcing methodologies used by organisations monitoring killings, such as Syria Tracker, during the Syrian conflict can effectively capture variations in conflict intensity over time. https://link.springer.com/article/10.1007%2Fs10610-014-9244-8
- Mariane Pearl, 'Syria Tracker: Women Dying in Numbers', Huff Post, 3 December 2015. 'Unsurprisingly, patterns show a steady rise in the proportion of female deaths over the course of the conflict. It went from less than one per cent in April 2011 to over eighteen per cent today suggesting targeted killing.' https://www.huffingtonpost.com/mariane-pearl/syria-tracker-women-dying_b_8710524.html
- Hala Gorani, 'Tracking Violence Against Women in Syria', CNN, 10 January 2013. https://www.cnn.com/videos/world/2013/01/10/idesk-intv-tracking-violence-against-women-in-syria.cnn

Notes

1. https://syriatracker.crowdmap.com (accessed on 17 March 2020).
2. Syria Tracker; Crowdsourcing Crisis Information. https://www.slideshare.net/humanitariantracker/syria-tracker-crowdsourcing-crisis-information (accessed on 17 March 2020).
3. How Syria Tracker Uses Data Mining and Machine Learning Methods to Uncover Civilian Targeted Events from the War in Syria. Video available at: https://vimeo.com/106284800 (accessed on 17 March 2020).
4. 51.2 per cent of the global population, or 3.9 billion people, were estimated to be using the Internet by end of 2018, ITU. https://www.itu.int/en/ITU-D/Statistics/Pages/stat/default.aspx (accessed on 17 March 2020).
5. http://www.data4sdgs.org/index.php/partner/humanitarian-tracker (accessed on 17 March 2020).

References

Alston, Philip and Sarah Knuckey. *The Transformation of Human Rights Fact-finding*. New York: Oxford University Press, 2016.

Dardagan, Hamit and Hana Salama. *Stolen Futures: The Hidden Death Toll of Child Casualties in Syria*. London: Oxford Research Group, 2013. http://www.everycasualty.org/downloads/reports/Stolen-Futures.pdf (accessed on 17 March 2020).

Finch, Kathryn C., Kassandra R. Snook, Isaac Chun-Hai Fung et al. 'Public Health Implications of Social Media Use During Natural Disasters, Environmental Disasters, and Other Environmental Concerns'. *Natural Hazards* 83, no. 1 (2016): 729–760.

Gjøsæter T. and Jaziar Radianti. 'Evaluating Accessibility and Usability of an Experimental Situational Awareness Room'. In *Advances in Design for Inclusion*, edited by Di Bucchianico G. International Conference on Applied Human Factors and Ergonomics 2018. *Advances in Intelligent Systems and Computing* 1, no. 776. Cham: Springer, 2019.

Goth, Greg. 'Crowdsourcing Platforms Monitor Disease, Dissent and Disasters'. Association for Computing Machinery. 8 March 2013. http://cacm.acm.org/news/161886-crowdsourcing-platforms-monitor-disease-dissent-and-disasters/fulltext (accessed on 17 March 2020).

Gutiérrez, Miren. *Data Activism and Social Change*. Cham, Switzerland: Palgrave Pivot, 2018, pp. 107–136.

Hubrecht, Joël. 'Syria: Is Justice Out of Reach?' *Esprit*, no. 6 (2017): 44–56.

Humanitarian Tracker: Crowdsourcing Syria Crisis Since 2011. https://reliefweb.int/report/syrian-arab-republic/humanitarian-tracker-crowdsourcing-syria-crisis-2011 (accessed on 17 March 2020).

Jewell, Nicholas P., Michael Spagat and Britta L. Jewell. 'Accounting for Civilian Casualties: From the Past to the Future'. *Social Science History* 42, no. 3 (2018): 1–32.

Kass-Hout, Taha A. and Hend Alhinnawi. 'Social Media in Public Health'. *British Medical Bulletin* 108, no. 1 (2013): 5–24.

Kass-Hout, Taha and Xiaohui Zhang, *Biosurveillance: Methods and Case Studies*. Boca Raton, FL: CRC Press, 2010.

Livingston, Steven and Jonathan Drake. 'We Tried to Save 150 People in Aleppo from 5,000 Miles Away'. *The Washington Post*, 9 January 2017. https://www.washingtonpost.com/news/monkey-cage/wp/2017/01/09/we-tried-to-save-150-people-in-aleppo-from-5000-miles-away (accessed on 17 March 2020).

Rall, Katharina, Margaret L. Satterthwaite, Anshul Vikram Pandey, John Emerson, Jeremy Boy, Oded Nov, Enrico Bertini. 'Data Visualisation for Human Rights Advocacy'. *Journal of Human Rights Practice* 8, no. 2 (2016): 171–197. (DOI: 10.1093/jhuman/huw011) https://academic.oup.com/jhrp/article-lookup/doi/10.1093/jhuman/huw011 (accessed on 17 March 2020) ['Crowdsourced human rights information is submitted by witnesses, survivors, and advocates and presented on interactive maps that are increasingly influential in policy circles because they allow viewers to explore data in near real time.']

Red Cross Red Crescent, Issue 1, 2014. https://www.icrc.org/eng/assets/files/publications/1141-red-cross-magazine-eng-1-2014.pdf (accessed on 17 March 2020).

Rogstadius, Jakob. *Enhancing Disaster Situational Awareness Through Scalable Curation of Social Media* (Unpublished PhD Thesis, University of Madeira, 2015).

Sarfaty, Galit A. 'Can Big Data Revolutionise International Human Rights Law'. *University of Pennsylvania Journal of International Law* 39, no. 1 (2017): 73-101.

Shiel, Annie. Conflict Crowdsourcing: Harnessing the Power of Crowdsourcing for Organisations Working in Conflict and the Potential for a Crowdsourced Portal for Conflict-related Information (Unpublished Thesis, 2013).

Standards for Casualty Recording, Every Casualty, Oxford University, 2016. http://www.everycasualty.org/downloads/ec/pdf/StandardsforCasualtyRecording-Version1.0(2016).pdf

Tomaszewski, Brian. *Geographic Information Systems (GIS) for Disaster Management*. Boca Raton, FL: CRC Press, 2014.

Ushahidi. 'The Story of Syria Tracker and Child Killing Trends in Syria'. 23 February 2015. https://www.ushahidi.com/blog/2015/02/23/the-story-of-syria-tracker-child-killing-trends-in-syria (accessed on 17 March 2020).

3

MAPPING FORGOTTEN PLACES AROUND THE WORLD (MISSING MAPS)

Interview with Jan Böhm, by Siddharth Peter de Souza

Could you tell us a bit about Missing Maps and what kind of work you do with the project?

Missing Maps is a joint initiative founded by Médecins Sans Frontières/ Doctors Without Borders (MSF), American and British Red Cross and Humanitarian OpenStreetMap Team (HOT). It addresses common challenges that humanitarians face in many areas. Even though it is 2019, a surprising number of people are not visible on any map. This is particularly the case of people living in areas affected by natural disasters and other emergencies. When we arrive on the ground, it is difficult to help people if we do not know where they are.

I work at MSF and my role in the project is to support volunteer communities that we have around the world. I am based in the Czech Republic where we have one of the biggest Missing Maps communities in the world. With thousands of volunteers and more than eighty mapping parties (mapathons) organised in the past three years, Czech Republic gives a nice example of how to grow a community; and my colleagues from all around the world turn to us when planning their own mapathons. This is the story of my position in Missing Maps.

Besides supporting Missing Maps volunteer communities at MSF, I also work on bringing stories of how mapping helped in the field. The impact of Missing Maps is widely positive and appreciated in practice. And we want to show it to those who help us.

How did the Missing Maps project come to be and what were the main objectives? Are there particular experiences or frameworks that shaped these ideas?

The Missing Maps initiative was founded in November 2014 and I joined MSF just after that. At MSF, we provide medical care to people who cannot reach it for many reasons. Often, the reasons are that they are trapped in a conflict or an area affected by natural disasters. However, sometimes people just cannot reach medical care because no one knows where they are.

I remember a story of my colleague who was working in South Kivu as a part of the emergency response team in early 2018, ready to be deployed whenever they receive a report from the local community or authorities. She told me that one day a mother came with two children, sick with measles. One of them died eventually. She said they were from a village, but this village was not on any maps. The team asked for advice, but received confusing information from the local community—some said the village is at a one-day walking distance, others said three. Also the directions varied. Internet connection was poor, satellite imagery was not an option and the team was not able to plan a trip, evaluate the security situation and pick the right means of transport. They even did not know where to go exactly. Eventually, they had to take a decision not to respond. This is a very painful experience, but sadly not unique.

Maps are crucial for our work. And we know that we cannot wait for commercial companies because they would not prioritise mapping rural areas in sub-Saharan Africa as against mapping regions where they have more customers.

The OpenStreetMap is a game changer for us. We can ask volunteers who can easily help with mapping. We can pick an area of interest and have a map of it in days or even hours.

When I first met Missing Maps, I was interested in finding an easy way to involve people in Czech Republic who were interested in supporting MSF. Missing Maps looked like a perfect solution: it was meaningful, easy-to-do and an open project. Anyone could learn it quickly and it brought real value to our operations.

I am working in humanitarian aid for more than ten years now, with a particular focus on digital tools. And I have never seen such a great initiative, a perfect combination of simplicity for contributors and real value for those who are using the data.

What were the types of data sources that you used? Did you encounter any difficulties using them?

Mapping consists of two main parts: remote mapping and field mapping. Before remote mapping is done by Missing Maps volunteers, GIS officers in the field had to collect data themselves. Having the Missing Maps support saves hours of their time every day. And time is usually what we do not have during emergencies.

Field mapping is crucial and we cannot skip it. You do not see the names of villages or wells on satellite imagery; also, you do not see what the buildings are used for. These information are important but are only available through field mapping.

However, doing mapping in the field costs time, money and can be dangerous sometimes. Saving a big part of it, thanks to the Missing Maps volunteers, means a lot to us.

When we do not have any maps, we often have to rely on hand-drawn maps. These help us identify villages where patients come from. Sometimes it happens that there are more than one village with the same name, so we need to ask patients for landmarks, such as if the village is next to a river or close to another village. Having a hand-drawn map is very helpful, but you cannot do an epidemiological analysis with a hand-drawn map, neither can you plan the logistics of a vaccination campaign.

How did you build a community around the project as an open-source map? How have you maintained an interest in the project?

In Czech Republic, we emphasise that Missing Maps is an open project made by volunteers. We avoid presenting mapathons as an event organised for volunteers to come and map. Instead, we present mapathons as an event organised by volunteers; therefore, we invite them to contribute in all parts of the process, from mapping to organising the party. We design mapathons as a regular meeting and a social event (see Figure 3.1). A true mapping party.

For me personally, the goal was to have a group of people who come to a mapathon without their computers. This is not to say I would like to put the focus away from mapping. It is good that most of the people come with their laptops and map. However, the fact that there is a small group of people who find it useful to come even if they are not mapping, is an indication of a living community. This is what I have seen in London, where we have one of the biggest mapathon communities. When the mapathon became a place where people like to come just to meet the others, speak about their fields of expertise, discuss the future development of OpenStreetMap, JOSM mapping plugins and other ideas, it was a dream come true for me.

At the moment, it is only me from MSF who is organising mapathons in Czech Republic and Slovakia. Everything else is being run by volunteers. In most of the cities outside the capital, volunteers are running mapathons completely on their own. In my opinion, the biggest success of our local Missing Maps community is the fact that the team of volunteers changed three times completely. People contributed actively, then their lives changed and they handed over their parts to someone else. But the community lives and continues. While we have contributed a lot to (not only) MSF operations, I find the sustainability of our community to be the real success.

To achieve this, we focused on opening as many small tasks as possible, from checking attendees list at the door to announcing the opening of registrations on the Missing Maps website or giving various training. Most of the tasks are quite easy, so anyone can sign up for them.

As the main communication channel, we have a Facebook group for all Czech and Slovak mapathons. In this group, people announce their mapathons as well as post questions about mapping and share interesting articles. For me (and for MSF), it presents a good channel to activate volunteers in case of emergency. For the 'core team' of volunteers—that is, those who do anything else than 'just' mapping—we have a Trello. There we have cards for new ideas and planned mapathons. In these cards, there are detailed checklists with all necessary tasks that need to be done for a mapathon. We regularly evaluate the Trello board to make sure it stays open and clear for someone who just meets the community for the first time. By doing this, we avoid becoming a closed group, unattractive for anyone new.

Tells us a little about the responses that the project has received? Who were the audiences? Have other organisations or groups reached out to use or build on it in particular ways?

Before I organised my first mapathon in Prague, I went to London to see how it looks like. To be honest, I was expecting a bunch of geeks doing something weird on their home-made machines that no one else could understand. At London, a lady of my grandmother's age came and sat next to me. She was no geek. She just had time and zest, learned mapping in a few minutes and did a great job for the humanitarian teams.

Over the past three years, I saw hundreds of people on our mapathons. There are three main groups that stand out. First one is a group of people who are mainly attracted to the technology. They do not necessarily care about humanitarian aid, but they like maps, either as a hobby or because they are GIS professionals. Mapping on a mapathon is interesting for them because it is a rare opportunity to create a map from scratch, to map something that has never been mapped before.

The second group are people who are mainly attracted to volunteering and doing something good. Missing Maps provides them with an easy way to do something meaningful, with a clear impact and no particular demands for skills.

The third group are people interested in becoming field-workers with MSF (or another humanitarian organisation, as many of them are members of the Missing Maps initiative now). They know they do not meet the requirements yet (mostly students), but they want to see MSF in action already. Mapathons are a great way for them to get us known.

In the end, mapathons put together a broad variety of people who would not meet otherwise. And by mapping something together, they get to know each other, develop new friendships, and after a while, they start coming to the mapathons just to see the others and spend a nice time together.

For me personally, mapathons are almost a therapeutic experience. Working at MSF is hard work sometimes, but being in a room full of people, who are like you, who want to actively support you and are interested in what you are doing, is an extremely strong positive experience.

What was the most challenging practical or conceptual aspects of building and working with Missing Maps?

Editing OpenStreetMap is easy to learn, and Missing Maps attracts many beginners. This is a positive sign; however, it also brings the concern of the quality of the data. To avoid mistakes and errors, validators are involved. These validators are experienced mappers who have mapped enough to identify a mistake quickly. But it takes time to have enough experience to become a validator. So ensuring good quality of the data is the main challenge in Missing Maps.

To train new validators, we need people to come repeatedly to mapathons. To keep them coming, we offer a 'ladder of experience'. On their first mapathon, volunteers only map with the most basic tool. Then they can sign up for JOSM, a much more convenient but also more complex mapping editor. When they feel confident enough, they can take a validator training and check the work of others.

What are the goals for Missing Maps and the team, going forward?
While all Missing Maps members and volunteers strive to provide data of increasing quality, improving the workflow is a particularly difficult challenge. Progress in AI (artificial intelligence) and machine learning presents an interesting opportunity for Missing Maps. The idea that volunteers on mapathons could be replaced by computers is, however, still more a wish than a reality. Image recognition can help with automated mapping, but it only works with high-resolution satellite imagery. The imagery available for Missing Maps is usually not that good. During the first trials of using image recognition when mapping the Kutupalong camp in Bangladesh, it came out that it takes more time to correct errors made by the automated system than to map it entirely manually.

Yet, the potential of AI and machine learning is big, and we are looking for ways to use it, regardless of the failures. So far, it seems like we do not have to look for the end of mapathons. The use of automated tools might reinforce the efforts of volunteers, so mapathons might still have a place, even if the contents of it changed.

Another new area is, moving more and more towards local data collection. We do this with the help of our MSF staff and local volunteer communities in the places we work. In countries like Zimbabwe or Bangladesh, there are today small groups of volunteers who organise mapathons and data collection to support our MSF activities. During Cyclone Idai, it was the Zimbabwe chapter of the Missing Maps volunteers that immediately started mapping their own country affected by the natural disaster. By supporting these local mappers in their activities and collecting more and better data in areas where there are no communities yet (like the Central African Republic or South Sudan), the OpenStreetMap database becomes richer with local information, and more useful.

Figure 3.1: A mapper digitising buildings on satellite imagery during a mapathon in Avast offices in Prague, August 2017. Photo by Josef Havlín (Left). Volunteers at the Missing Maps mapathon in Opero coworking place, Prague, listen to the introduction from Jan Böhm, MSF Missing Maps community coordinator, October 2017. Photo by MSF (right).

PART II

CONTESTED TERRITORIES

4

PLACING SEGREGATION

Rob Shepard

Introduction

Residential segregation is the literal separation of humanity—social groups divided and driven apart spatially by arbitrary characteristics. While some of the humanistic and experiential elements of such inequality can be captured in photographs, stories, or discussions, the full extent of residential segregation is also something that can be studied scientifically, demonstrated to audiences and used as an educational tool. What does it mean, though, to communicate that a city is or was 'moderately segregated', or to report that there is a high 'dissimilarity index' between the white and non-white population across a city's neighbourhoods? These descriptions have value in establishing the intensity of the issue, but they do not show audiences where or how a city is divided or who was affected, and the measurements themselves can be somewhat arbitrary. Visualisations of the underlying empirical data can be a very powerful communication tool and a radical form of education on the topic. Such visualisations have long been used in related scholarship. In his work *The Philadelphia Negro*, for example, W.E.B. Du Bois famously collected and mapped highly granular data on individual households for his sociological study of social problems facing the Black community of Philadelphia's Seventh Ward in the late 1890s. Maps such as those created by Du Bois quickly show audiences meaningful patterns and inequalities across the landscape, and contemporary interactive maps that enable a user to zoom, layer and query data have substantially more potential to inform.

Placing Segregation is an initial effort to connect audiences with highly detailed household-level spatial data on all residents of select major cities for the years 1860 and 1870, to the furthest extent possible. The following sections introduce the basics of the project, including its data sources, choices, challenges and importance within the realm of segregation studies and digital scholarship.

Context for the Project

For the study of residential segregation in American cities, records collected by the United States Bureau of the Census and the publishers of city directories are sufficiently rife with information about individuals and families, and these details can be used to link highly detailed data to particular locations across history. Unfortunately, accessing the highest detail from these potential datasets is exceptionally challenging and labour intensive, as much of the built environment has changed with time, including re-routing, renumbering and even renaming of streets, buildings and other places of interest. More importantly, simple location details such as addresses—the most important and detailed piece of spatial identity in the census—were not even part of the standard population census questions until 1880 (United States Bureau of the Census 1997; DeBats 2008). While quality urban histories already exist for many large American cities, there have been fewer efforts to locate and analyse individuals and all available household-level census data before the very end of the 19th century.

Some of the most notable quantitative studies of urban segregation patterns that trace the roots and history of the phenomenon turn to the analysis of aggregate data, such as evaluating the count of citizens by race at the level of city wards. As the Census Bureau was publishing data about race at the level of city wards, the practice of using city wards has been typically employed in many empirical studies of 19th- and early 20th-century cities, inevitably creating studies that are 'misleading about the level of segregation, a lacuna that was evident to researchers who looked beyond census sources' (Logan and Martinez 2018). In their influential work *American Apartheid*, for example, Douglas Massey and Nancy Denton note that people of colour only 'rarely' exceeded 30 per cent of the population in any area within a city (Massey and Denton 1993, 20). However, American cities were smaller in population and denser, especially before the adoption of the car, and it is somewhat unrealistic to assume that residential segregation was neatly confined within arbitrary government boundaries where it would be measurable across large unit areas. Ward-level maps of

Chicago in 1900, for example, appear to show African Americans living all over the city even though it was common knowledge that they were clustering disproportionately in the city's south side during that same time (Philpott 1978; Logan, Zhang and Chunyu 2015). Recent scholarship on historical residential segregation likewise notes that low segregation indices in southern US cities are mainly a function of the scale and spatial configuration of places, masking 'a substantial degree of segregation even within small residential areas' (Logan and Martinez 2018). In the absence of household-level spatial data on socio-economic conditions before 1880, a thorough understanding of microscale urban patterns and residential segregation is missing from a critical urban development period in American history.

Additionally, infamous historical processes of *de jure* residential segregation, such as restrictive covenants, redlining and 'Jim Crow' laws are more visible and direct means of maintaining physical separation among racial and ethnic groups, therefore, they are stronger in public memory. However, these are products of the late 19th century and 20th century, and they developed primarily as white supremacists sought to reassert complete control over spaces, especially in the wake of Emancipation and subsequent Reconstruction. Earlier decades provide insight into how cities looked even before these mechanisms were deployed. Despite their free status, the free Black population still had very little power in American society into the middle 19th century, completely banned from basic education in many places and—with notable exceptions among groups of skilled Black tradesmen—often forced to compete with the influx of immigrant labourers (Frazier 1932). This makes pre-1880 studies of residential segregation even more compelling: they reflect a time in which free Black Americans existed alongside a race-based system of slavery.

About Placing Segregation

Placing Segregation is a move to begin filling this void by revealing to audiences what residential segregation patterns actually looked like in large, developing American cities before the end of the

19th century, identifying who specifically was impacted by making visible their names and conditions. To the fullest extent possible, the project geolocates every family in 19th century American cities, beginning with the years 1860 and 1870, two decennial census years in which the US Census Bureau had collected detailed economic information about individuals, such as personal estate wealth and value of real estate holdings before these questions were omitted from subsequent censuses.

In its most nascent phase, the project started merely as an effort to create a new map layer to accompany the Civil War Washington project. Professor Kenneth Winkle of the University of Nebraska History Department had been studying demographics of the city of Washington's diverse First Ward in 1860, and he had painstakingly transcribed and matched census records from that ward with individuals' city directory entries to derive location information. Meanwhile, Dr Elizabeth Lorang, University of Nebraska Digital Humanities librarian and project manager, had acquired period city directories that included comprehensive street directories for the city to help match historical addresses of various items with their contemporary locations. Working as a graduate assistant and GIS Specialist for the project in 2012 and drawing from these primary sources, I developed an address locator system in ArcGIS to automatically geolocate historical addresses for the city, batch processing Professor Winkle's initial dataset as my first test of the system. The geocoded census records provided a more nuanced understanding of residential segregation in the ward at the time, namely demonstrating the physical separation between white and free Black households as well as the intense clustering of wealthy white landowners along major thoroughfares in what otherwise might have appeared to be a more diverse ward (Shepard 2015). Those first findings helped to write the book on a specific part of the City of Washington, but more importantly, the experience highlighted the potential application of that process to the rest of the city as well as other major American cities. I then dove into a six-year effort to acquire, transcribe and geolocate tens of thousands of historical records, aided by transcription assistance from student workers Annie Klusak and Greg McKee as well as Digital Project Librarian Justin Baumgartner at the University of Iowa Libraries.

Initially, Placing Segregation has geolocated all available families and their associated census information, identifying each by the head of household, for the cities of Washington, D.C. and Nashville, Tennessee in 1860 and Omaha, Nebraska for the year 1870. These places have been selected to represent a geographic and economic balance of American cities during this formative period. By geolocating every family in historical records along with their associated data, we have both situated tens of thousands of individuals in their historical context for additional exploratory research, and we have built a highly detailed point map of information that is not dependent on arbitrary political boundaries and other changeable unit areas. This enables researchers to explore socio-economic changes across very small areas like city blocks (see Figures 4.1 and 4.2).

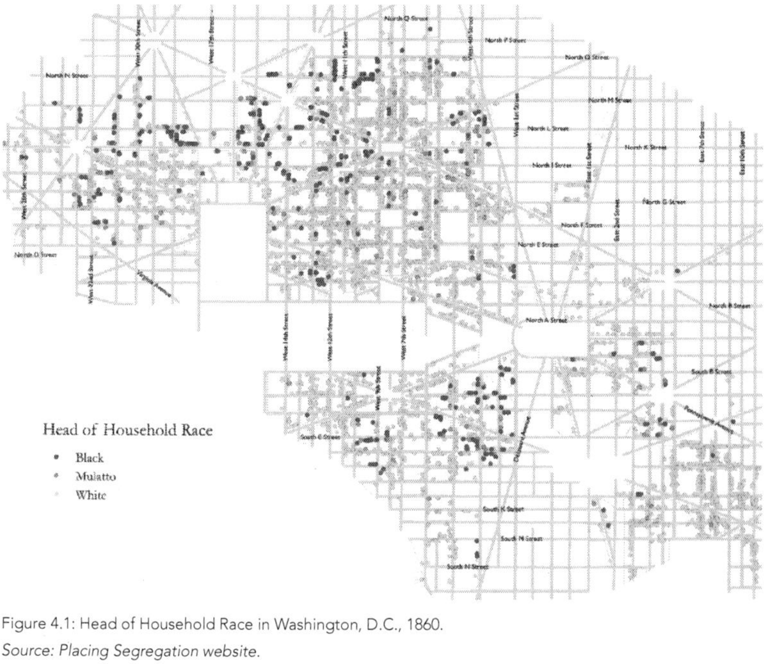

Figure 4.1: Head of Household Race in Washington, D.C., 1860.
Source: Placing Segregation website.

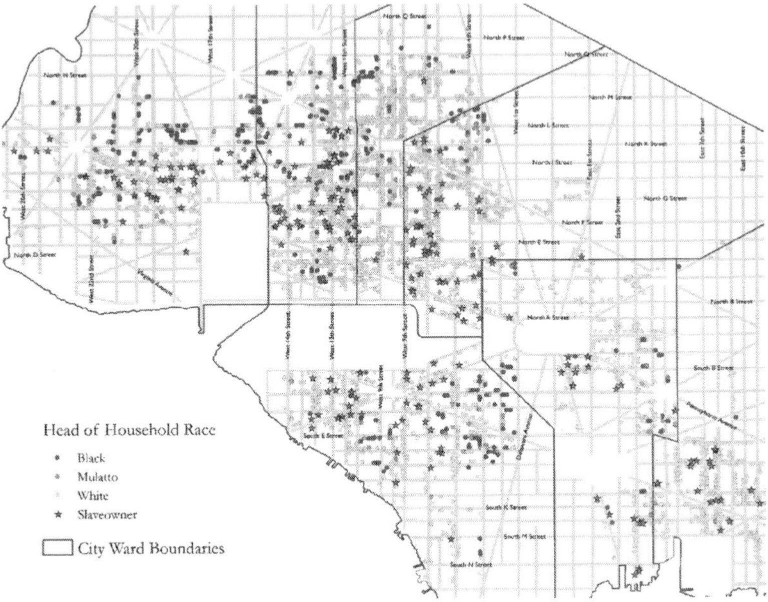

Figure 4.2: Race and Ward Boundaries in Washington, D.C., 1860.
Source: Placing Segregation website.

Sources

Placing Segregation maps such data from census records as a person's first and last names, historical address, occupation, the value of the family's personal estate, the value of the family's real estate and race according to the census taker. Likely slaveholders are also identified and mapped in the project, however, not merely to document their locations. While the inclusion of slaveholders helps to illustrate the pervasiveness of human bondage in developing American cities, their presence is more important for indicating those people who are otherwise underrepresented. Due to the Congressional 'three-fifths compromise', which allowed states to count 60 per cent of slaves toward their population for purposes of apportionment, the federal government required a slave census in addition to the regular census of population (Anderson, Citro and Salvo 2012). Enslaved men and women, treated as human property, were in almost all instances neither given names nor evaluated on their conditions. They were, however, enumerated and listed by their age, sex and owner name (Anderson 2015; United States Bureau of the Census 1860). Because it was common and, in places like

Washington, legally required for slaves to live at the property of their masters, including the locations of slaveholders is a primary way to locate and represent those enslaved men and women who are otherwise missing from the map.

Primary data sources for this project are the manuscript United States Census records, historical maps of cities during the period 1860–1870 and the historical city directories detailing the house numbering system and residents' addresses or locations relative to cross streets. It was necessary to use both census records and city directory records because the 1880 census was the first to begin collecting respondents' addresses; there is no direct connection between American census records and exact locations before that year. For the study of the City of Washington, *Boyd's Washington and Georgetown Directory* (1860) identifies names and occupations, while the 1865 edition of the directory from the same publisher provides additional street numbering information at each intersection to replicate Washington's house numbering system. Albert Boschke's 'Map of Washington City, District of Columbia, seat of the federal government', commissioned and developed in the 1850s and finalised in 1857, provides an extremely accurate large-scale map of the city, complete with property lines and building footprints to help further align house numbers and structures. The Nashville City and Business Directory for 1860–1861, published by L.P. Williams and Company, contains the full address and occupation information for that city's residents. Haydon and Booth's 1860 'City of Nashville and Edgefield' map provides more sufficient detail with which to identify individual lots and structures in the city at the time. Unfortunately, there are no descriptive street directories for the City of Nashville in relevant city directories. Omaha, too, did not have any description of the house numbering system in its period directory, residences are identified specifically in reference to street intersections. H.F. Greene produced the Map of the City of Omaha, 1870, a large-scale map of the city detailing all city streets, some of the city's numbered lots and, on the outskirts of development, it even included residents' names on farms and larger properties.

Methods

To begin, we manually transcribed and tabulated all available census records and each entry in the city directories into a spreadsheet and matched these individuals' first and last names and occupations from census records with the corresponding records listed in city directories to obtain address information and append it to the wealth of data present in the census. In theory, this method would produce perfect results, but it was necessary to make minor adjustments for thousands of records due to imperfect matches. Across all cities, matching census records with city directory records was made significantly more difficult because census takers did not verify name spellings. Apparently, no one was sacred to these census takers: even the Mayor of Washington at the time of the study, James G. Berret, ended up being spelt as 'James Barrett' (US Manuscript Census 1860). Notably, the city's mayor also was one of the dozens of Washingtonians who did not have any specific address identified by the city directory either, only a general description of his area of residence. Still, this type of ambiguous location description was often useful in the absence of detailed numbering information.

We made adjustments throughout the joining process to ensure high-quality matches even in the absence of perfect links. When occupations could be linked up and names in the census also matched phonetically to names in the city directory, we assumed these records to be properly linked. For instance, a barber named 'John Green' in the census was matched with a barber identified as 'John Greene' in the corresponding city directory. To add further integrity to this process, manuscript census pages already indicate city wards and we processed data ward by ward, so the positive identification linking census record to a city directory record also required a common first name and often a middle initial, a common last name, holding the same or highly similar occupation and even a general neighbourhood in common. With a few minor exceptions, virtually nobody outside of immediate family members shared the same names and occupation and ward, so this provided an additional check on possible mistakes by the census takers.

In order to reconstruct each city's street grid and orientation properly, we synthesised all available accurate historical base maps for Washington, Omaha and Nashville and georeferenced them to be aligned digitally with their physical locations and brought into desktop GIS software. We subsequently digitised street lines over these georeferenced base map images. Using city directories' descriptions of house numbering systems (usually the 'Street Directory' section) as an initial point of reference, we manually coded individual line segments in the centreline shapefile with starting and ending address numbers for each side of the street, which is intended to correspond to the historical address numbering system. Essentially, we built the same sort of address locator system used by something like Google Maps, but specific to this unique period.

Challenges of Data Collection

The process of using city directories and old maps to build a historical address locator, however, presents a number of challenges. In particular, the formal records of the city directory provided some initial limitations for reconstructing the street grid and numbering patterns. While the city of Washington directory had a street directory listing exact building numbers at each major intersection, the other two study areas had more complicated situations. The city of Omaha's sources incidentally listed some resident address numbers at the 'corner' of a cross street, which allowed for many points of interpolation to make sense of its grid. Nashville's city directories for the period never elaborated on its numbering system, and yet nearly all residents were identified by house numbers in the city directories. Fortunately, dozens of business advertisements from Nashville city directories during the period 1853–1868 listed store locations relative to cross streets, for example, listing a business at 64 south college street as 'second door from Broad [Street]' (L.P. Williams and Co. 1861). Ultimately, these points became references for building an address locator system for the three cities.

Until the late 19th century, many cities also did not use standardised numbering systems for buildings and houses. Address numbers on urban blocks initially were not sensibly divided into common ranges by cross streets: where today a visitor walking among address numbers ascending through the 200 range would reasonably expect to find address numbers in the 300 range beginning after the next intersection, major American cities like Washington D.C. did not use that logic until the late 19th century. Addresses often ascended based on lots and existing buildings, which varied in size and density across the city, meaning that the number of the first building after an intersection was dependent entirely on 'earlier' parts of the street. Notably, the City of Philadelphia was just introducing its logical 'block' system of numbering in the late 1850s, which eventually would serve as a model for other cities in the late 19th century (Rose-Redwood 2008). Publishers and city officials consequently worked to develop city directories that included the addresses of services and individuals across the city and likewise explained the 'orientation' and origin of street numbers so that those who purchased the directory could navigate the numbering system and find services.

While city directories collected a wide variety of names and occupations, they were at times selective about who was included (Rose-Redwood 2008). Men, most often the heads of household, dominate the pages of directories used in this project, while women were typically only listed if they were widows, keepers of boarding houses, those who provided particular services such as washing clothing, or were otherwise the head of a household. Historians also have noted that city directories underrepresented the Black population in southern cities, particularly with respect to poorer Black families (Rabinowitz 1978, 344). In the most egregious example of shortcomings with the city directories discovered by this research effort, the entire 1860 city directory for Nashville lists only some thirty people of colour. Omaha's 1870 directory likewise notes that the publisher took every effort to obtain names of all who 'should' appear in a city directory, without specifying what criteria are used to make such a judgment (Boyd 1860). The extent or purpose of any publisher's omissions might never be determined, however, it certainly limits who might be included in subsequent datasets.

Moreover, despite efforts to count all individuals, census records themselves are neither neutral nor unbiased. This issue impacts even contemporary data: drawing from other sources such as birth records to compare numbers, researchers have found that as many as one million young children were missing entirely even from the 2010 census, and minority children are most at risk for undercount in the census (United States Bureau of the Census 2014). Furthermore, the undercount rate among Black Americans was roughly 2 per cent in both the 2000 and 2010 censuses, driven in large part by particularly high rates of undercount among middle-aged Black men (United States Bureau of the Census 2012). While the modern census statisticians may use substitution and imputation to attempt to derive a more accurate count of those who are missed, that process does not replace those individuals whose entries are now missing from the official record. Consequently, the likelihood is that many people are simply missing from historical datasets. Among those missing are not only those who were enslaved and given only their owners' names as a reference but also the extremely poor and transient populations who were often missed by census takers. Francis Walker, the superintendent of the 1870 census, claimed in official testimony that the 'censuses of 1850, 1860 and of 1870 are loaded with bad statistics', and suggested that results in some extreme cases were only 'half' correct (United States Congress, Senate 1878). Characteristics such as home accessibility, voter registration and whether or not a person owned property all increased the likelihood of being included in the census (Steckel 1991). Census records certainly are not infallible, but they are among the best available sources of information historically, as documentation like tax rolls were even less inclusive (DeBats 2008).

Design Choices

Displaying the data in the form of an interactive map was a deliberate choice, an effort to take a positive step towards visibility. Not only are maps critically important instruments of communication for spatial phenomena like residential locations, but historical residential segregation—particularly for this relatively early period in American urban history—is something that can be diluted or hidden entirely without a point map of available data. Scholars of American urban history have noted, for example, that residential clustering of marginalised minority groups could be present along back alleys or side streets very near to white residences in physical space but entirely separate in social space and visibility from main streets (Logan and Martinez 2018; Massey and Denton 1993). These patterns, which certainly do appear in all of the project's existing study areas, would not be fully accessible to audiences without a true point map.

Finally, to ensure widespread usability, a very simple map interface is used. Existing literature has noted that interactive map users without GIS experience exhibit difficulty interpreting overly complex data visualisations such as numerous map icons and layers (Newman et al. 2010). Therefore, rather than providing dozens of layers to manage, data are made available as one single layer on the map. The site's user interface provides all geocoded census records as points that, when clicked, generate pop-up windows with complete information about each head of household living at that location, along with the aggregated estate values for that individual's family. Each person's address or specific location as recorded in the city directories is also listed in the pop-up windows. Listing each address highlights the extent of differences between the historical street grid and the contemporary system, and although these data have been checked thoroughly for accuracy, it also provides a requisite level of transparency that will enable other experts to identify, document and notify the project of any possible issues with locations of individuals.

The tools for filtering and using data are also designed to promote ease of use. A search tool on the top left of the screen allows visitors to type in a name to search for a particular individual. Using the power of a Fuse.js, an open JavaScript library, users can type in the information for a 'fuzzy search' (one that quickly generates suggestions and similar results to what they are typing into the text-box in real time) with this tool. Even if site visitors do not know a particular name or its proper spelling in the census records, the search feature will calculate the most likely candidates based on the letters that have been entered, and put those results at the top of a list. Likewise, a basic radio button menu, displayed prominently on the upper right-hand side of the screen, gives users the ability to filter data for various groups of interest. Each city map has been populated with unique layers for people of colour, immigrants from Ireland, immigrants from German territories and states, merchants of all types, labourers and 'elites' defined as bankers, lawyers and gentlemen. These categories are directly associated with the variables used for spatial comparison of various groups. When one of the categories in the filter is selected by a user, all of the dots with individuals who fit that specific criterion appear to highlight themselves immediately as a bright yellow layer that sits on top of the base layer for all residents, providing a quick reference to all of their locations and allowing users to click directly on individuals in the group of interest to obtain more information. Also, this feature allows site visitors to create custom map visualisations of the distribution of various groups. For example, a researcher inspecting the spatial distribution of people of colour in Washington, D.C. can get a quick map of all of their locations in 1860 by clicking on the 'People of Colour' category.

In addition to making the interface simple enough for a broad variety of prospective users, the code for the site is also as basic as possible to help ensure digital preservation and long term compatibility with web browsers. Everything has been written with free and open source components and created with simple HTML, CSS and JavaScript functions. Rather than storing the geographic data in a proprietary format or as map layer files that are native to a specific GIS program, data layers are stored as text-based GeoJSON files. These are JavaScript Object Notation files, which tell web browsers how to interpret and use any attributes associated with each object, and they include an additional field to describe the geography of each object as points, lines or areas in basic Cartesian coordinates. Anybody with a web browser or text editor can view and access these GeoJSON files from this project directly as text files, edit them at will and even upload them to their web server if desired. They are listed in a downloads section for people who might want to do that. Furthermore, the more advanced scripts used in the map code itself are drawn from the popular open-source Leaflet.js, a JavaScript library designed for basic mapping applications.

Conclusion and Next Steps

Widespread accessibility and adaptability are paramount to the spirit of this project, as we recognise how dynamic web mapping that is responsive to viewers has enabled new possibilities for communicating with audiences. Our ability to study historical inequalities and their relationship to the present in high detail is not bound by existing maps or narratives. Placing Segregation demonstrates that we can develop unique, historically accurate spatial data by synthesising sources, creating new perspectives and new tools through contemporary mapping technologies. Together with similar emerging digital humanities projects like the Urban Transition Historical GIS Project at Brown University and University of Richmond's Mapping Inequality: Redlining in New Deal America, which aim to expand our knowledge of historical segregation and its effect on modern cities, Placing Segregation hopes to bring about a positive change in the way that we understand the histories of inequality. Human geographers have at present a responsibility to rethink our relationship with our spatial datasets so that we are not only crafting arguments from available information but also generating new data and new ways for others to interact with it.

In creating this site, the expectation is that other scholars will utilise these datasets in their own related urban historical geographies, submit modifications to arguments or data provided here, or use the information from the site to contribute to the larger scholarly discussion about these cities and other places. The project was first introduced at the Digital Humanities 2017 Conference in Montreal, Quebec, and subsequently demonstrated with key findings the following year at the Annual Meeting of the American Association of Geographers in New Orleans, Louisiana. Since its introduction, Placing Segregation has been included among numerous subject guides for digital humanities and Black spatial history projects, and it was prominently featured in an October 2017 Forbes piece entitled 'How is Digital Mapping Changing the Way We Visualise Racism and Segregation?' The widest adoption so far, though, seems to be teachers using the material in the classroom. Because the map application is relatively straightforward, this digital edition provides a highly accessible and interactive means of educating students about urban history as well as the complexities of residential segregation more broadly. However, because the full datasets are also available for download and further analysis in GIS software, some faculty have reached out to mention that they are using these data in coursework. For example, Adam Sundberg, an Assistant Professor of History and Digital Humanities at Creighton University, noted that his Spring 2018 students were using these GIS data to study the history of residential segregation in Omaha. Indeed, Placing Segregation has made its way onto multiple university syllabi and research guides, and we are excited to see this list expand in future.

More importantly, this project contributes to contemporary discussions about ethnicity, race and control of space by digging deeper into the roots of residential segregation in cities. So far, the project demonstrates that African Americans—as well as immigrant groups like Irish and Germans to a lesser extent—already were significantly segregated from the native-born white population in cities as early as 1860. Even before racist policies like restrictive covenants sought to exclude minority groups from parts of cities, these groups were effectively excluded from large parts of urban places, quite possibly due to severe economic disadvantages; therefore, we ought to question narratives that introduce segregation as a problem that developed in the 20th century alone. Those policies that we associate with contemporary urban segregation might then be thought of as state-sponsored legal mechanisms for ensuring that social and physical separation continued beyond its nascent forms, enforceable in the face of great migrations and adjusted to suit 20th-century concepts of territoriality. We illustrate with these maps that exclusion historically is something that may be virtually invisible at conventional scales like wards and neighbourhoods. Finally, we are not merely visualising data for the sake of bolstering scholarly arguments: the points on the map do collectively represent patterns of exclusion, but each point on the map also corresponds to a person who lived through the social conditions we seek to study and represent. We hope that this project, by marrying large datasets on socio-economic variables with pieces of so many individual life stories, will re-emphasise the human element that underlies social science research.

References

Anderson, Margo J. *The American Census: A Social History*. New Haven, CT: Yale University Press, 2015.

Anderson, Margo J, Constance F. Citro and Joseph J. Salvo. 'Three-Fifths Compromise'. In *Encyclopaedia of the U.S. Census*. 2nd Edition. Washington, D.C.: CQ Press, 2012.

Boyd, William H. *Boyd's Washington and Georgetown Directory: Containing a Business Directory of Washington, Georgetown and Alexandria*. Washington, D.C.: Taylor and Maury, 1860.

DeBats, Donald. 'A Tale of Two Cities: Using Tax Records to Develop GIS Files for Mapping and Understanding Nineteenth-Century U.S. Cities'. *Historical Methods* 41, no. 1 (Winter 2008): 17–38.

Frazier, E. Franklin. *The Free Negro Family: A Study of Family Origins Before the Civil War*. Nashville, TN: Fisk University Press, 1932.

L.P. Williams and Co. *Nashville City and Business Directory for 1860–61*. Volume 5 (1861).

Massey, Douglas and Nancy A. Denton. *American Apartheid: Segregation and the Making of the Underclass*. Cambridge, MA: Harvard University Press, 1993.

Newman, Greg, Don Zimmarman, Alycia Crall, Melinda Laituri, Jim Graham and Linda Stapel. 'User-Friendly Web Mapping: Lessons from a Citizen Science Website'. *International Journal of Geographical Information Science* 24, 12 (2010): 1851–1869.

Philpott, Thomas Lee. *The Slum and the Ghetto: Neighborhood Deterioration and Middle-Class Reform, Chicago, 1880–1930*. New York: Oxford University Press, 1978.

Rabinowitz, Howard N. *Race Relations in the Urban South, 1865–1890*. New York: Oxford University Press, 1978.

Rose, James M. and Alice Eicholz. *Black Genesis: A Resource Book for African-American Genealogy*. Baltimore, MD: Genealogical Publishing Company, 2003.

Rose-Redwood, Reuben S. 'Indexing the Great Ledger of the Community: Urban House Numbering, City Directories, and the Production of Spatial Legibility'. *Journal of Historical Geography* 34, no. 2 (2008): 286–310.

Shepard, Rob. 'Historical Geography, GIS and Civil War Washington'. In *Civil War Washington: History, Place, and Digital Scholarship*, edited by Susan Lawrence, 35–54. Lincoln, NE: University of Nebraska Press, 2015.

Steckel, Richard. 'The Quality of Census Data for Historical Inquiry: A Research Agenda'. *Social Science History* 15, no. 4 (Winter 1991): 579–599.

United States Bureau of the Census. *Eighth Census of the United States, 1860*. Washington, D.C.: National Archives and Records Administration. United States of America, 1860.

United States Bureau of the Census. 'The Undercount of Young Children'. *Task Force Report: United States Department of Commerce, Economics and Statistics Administration*. Suitland, MD: United States Bureau of the Census, 2014. https://www.census.gov/content/dam/Census/library/working-papers/2014/demo/2014-undercount-children.pdf

United States Bureau of the Census. 'Census Bureau Releases Estimates of Undercount and Overcount in the 2010 Census'. Press Release (Public Information Office). Suitland, MD: United States Bureau of the Census, 2012. https://www.census.gov/newsroom/releases/archives/2010_census/cb12-95.html

United States Bureau of the Census. 'Availability of Census Records About Individuals'. *Factfinder for the Nation* 2. Rev. edition. Suitland, MD: United States Bureau of the Census, 1997. http://www.census.gov/prod/2/gen/cff/cff-9702.pdf

United States Bureau of the Census. '200 Years of Census Taking: Population and Housing Questions, 1790–1990'. Washington, D.C.: United States Government Printing Office 1989.

United States Congress, Senate. 'Interview of the select committees of the senate of the United States and of the House of Representatives to make provision for taking the tenth census'. *The Miscellaneous Documents of the Senate of the United States for the Third Session of the Forty Fifth Congress, 1878–1879*. Miscellaneous Document 26. Washington: US Government Printing Office, 1878.

Wolfe, J. M. *Omaha Directory for 1870*. Omaha, Nebraska: Omaha Daily Herald, 1870.

5

ARCHIVING VIOLENCE, UNDERSTANDING HATE IN SOUTH ASIA WITH INTOLERANCE TRACKER

Siddharth Peter de Souza, Saba Sharma, Nida Rehman and Nooreen Reza

Introduction

While South Asia is no stranger to the myriad ills of majoritarian prejudices, communal violence and suppression of dissent, in recent years, there have been increasing instances of hate crimes against minorities, silencing of critics, and increasing intolerance (Chaney and Sahoo 2020; Mander 2018; Nair 2018). In India, the suspected arson of St. Sebastian's Church in New Delhi in December is a case in point (McCarthy 2015). Only a few days later that same month, there was widespread outrage when the Hindu nationalist group, the Dharam Jagran Samanvay Vibhag, organised a mass conversion of predominantly poor Muslim families in Agra, by deception, to Hinduism, as part of its '*ghar wapsi*' or 'homecoming' campaign (Sahu 2015). The year 2015 began with the assassination of the secular, leftist activist Govind Pansare in February (Pandit 2015). This proved to be part of a trend of violence against secular, progressive intellectuals that continued with the killing of writer–activists M.M. Kalburgi and Gauri Lankesh (Scroll Staff 2019).

Perhaps the moment when not only India but the world was jolted into the realisation that something had gone deeply wrong in the country was the Dadri lynching of September 2015. On the night of 28 September, an elderly Muslim man, Muhammad Akhlaq, was dragged out of his home by a mob and brutally murdered on the pretence that he had killed a cow for its meat. The incident drew international attention (Shroff 2018). Unfortunately, it proved to be one of many more 'cow lynching' that followed. A report by Human Rights Watch states that 'Between May 2015 and December 2018, at least 44 people—36 of them Muslims—were killed across 12 Indian states' by the so-called cow vigilantes (Human Rights Watch 2019).

This drastic uptick in violence was not limited to India. In March 2015, a faction of the Pakistani Taliban bombed two churches in the Youhanabad neighbourhood of Lahore, an area of the city with a large Christian population (Akbar 2015). In April, the targeting of outspoken dissenters in India was mirrored in Pakistan with the murder of human rights activist Sabeen Mahmud (Boone 2015). Mass violence returned in May, when a group of gunmen went after the Ismaili community in a bus attack in the Safoora Goth neighbourhood of Karachi, killing at least forty-five people (BBC Staff 2015). In November, it was Ahmadis who were targeted in a two-day long pogrom in Punjab in Pakistan (Kayani 2015). Also, overall the South Asian Terrorism Portal found that an astonishing 251 people were killed and 316 injured in anti-Shia violence in the country in 2015 (Rizwi 2016). Meanwhile, across the subcontinent in Bangladesh, a series of attacks against atheist, secular bloggers and allied publishers that began in 2013 picked up steam with the murders of five people in 2015 alone (Tharoor 2016; Avijit Roy 2016). In early 2016, bigots in Bangladesh also claimed the lives of LGBTQ rights activists Xulhaz Mannan and Tanay Mojumdar (Xulhaz Mannan 2016).

This felt, at the moment, like a subcontinental conflagration. Numerous forces of hatred and intolerance, which had of course been a feature of political life in many South Asian nations, nevertheless seemed to coalesce and reflect across borders in ways that illuminated both their commonalities and the specific conditions of each country. In February 2016, according to reports by (Burke and agencies 2016) (Biswas 2016), after being accused by Akhil Bharatiya Vidyarthi Parishad (ABVP), the student wing of Bharatiya Janata Party (BJP), of making 'anti-national' statements at a rally, student leader Kanhaiya Kumar was arrested on charges of sedition. Six other students—Umar Khalid, Anirban Bhattacharya, Ashutosh Kumar, Anant Prakash Narayan, Riyazul Haq and Rama Naga—were also sought by police in the crackdown. The actions of the government sparked protests in Delhi and at other Indian universities; and by students, academics and public intellectuals around the world (The Wire Staff 2016).

It was not long after this campaign that we were inspired to start Intolerance Tracker, a mapping project meant to collect, categorise and archive the deluge of anti-minority and anti-democratic incidents taking place across the subcontinent (deSouza and Sharma 2016). It was important to us to cover all the countries of South Asia, to not only highlight the situations in individual countries but also reveal how these events may relate to each other and a broader political turn towards majoritarianism and targeted violence in the subcontinent (deSouza, Sharma and Rehman 2016; Bhawsar et al. 2017). The map was populated solely by volunteers, with each of us monitoring relevant media reports to add data to the map as information of intolerance became available. We also classified events in the map by the status and identities of victims and perpetrators, including categories such as caste, gender and religion (for victims), and by political groups, government actors and individuals (for perpetrators) (see Figure 5.1).

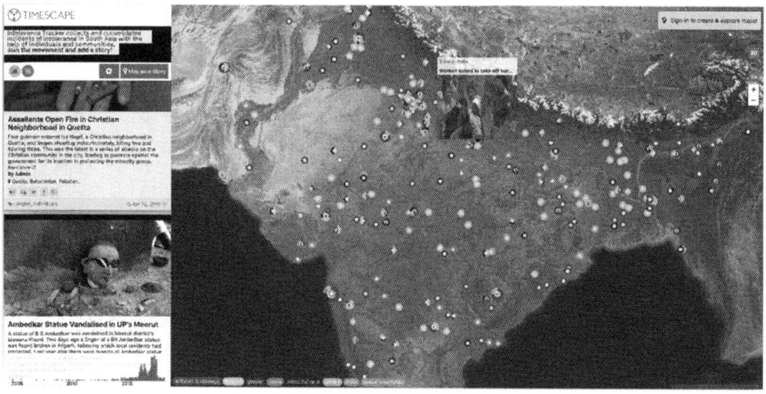

Figure 5.1: Events on the Intolerance Tracker map with details in the timeline on the sidebar.
Source: Intolerance Tracker website.

While we aimed to maintain Intolerance Tracker as record of hate crimes and violence from across South Asia and to create a knowledge-sharing platform to encourage accountability, other well-resourced outlets also took on a similar mission. However, these projects were limited to tracking intolerance in India only. Amnesty International debuted its Halt the Hate map to document incidents of hate crime from 28 September 2015 onwards, the date of the Dadri mob lynching of Muhammad Akhlaq. Halt the Hate organises its data by the identities of the victims and alleged motives; it also adds categories to document the types of attacks, the states in which they occur and the parties in power at the time of the incidents. In this way, the map helps to create a more detailed and organised picture of violence in India, and hopefully, a similar project in other South Asian countries will be pioneered successfully to facilitate the creation of comparative datasets (Halt the Hate n.d.).

While Halt the Hate is still going strong, other similar initiatives have met their abrupt ends. The *Hindustan Times*, one of India's most widely circulating English language newspapers, launched its own Hate Tracker in July 2017. It started collecting identity-based data of hate crimes and similar incidents from September 2015 via online crowdsourcing. However, the project lasted barely two months before it was removed from the site in October 2017 (The Wire Staff 2016). Whether the erasure of the Hate Tracker was due to internal deliberations in the newspaper or external pressure is still open to debate.

Very recently, in January 2019, one organisation started the task of turning crowdsourced hate-reporting into an accountability tool directed at the government. Citizens for Justice and Peace (CJP), a human rights advocacy group founded in 2002 after the anti-Muslim violence in Gujarat, launched the HateHatao app for Android. Writing in The Wire, CJP secretary and journalist Teesta Setalvad explained that anyone, a victim or a witness of a hate-motivated incident, can report her or his experience via the app, along with evidence in the form of photos or videos. From there, CJP will take these reports and send them 'to authorities such as the National Human Rights Commission (NHRC), the Press Council of India (PCI), the National Broadcasters Association (NBA), Facebook, Twitter and other social media platforms or law enforcement agencies' (Setalvad 2019). CJP also plans to pursue the most serious reports through the judicial system. CJP has been engaged for many years in efforts to collect reports of hate crimes, gender-based violence and state repression through its Peace Map initiative and other campaigns. HateHatao represents a new phase of this project, in which the data collected will not only form an information bank but also form the foundation of advocacy efforts to combat the further escalation of such incidents (Setalvad 2019).

These dynamics of violence in South Asia are also reflected globally in the United States, Brazil, the Philippines, the United Kingdom, Hungary, with the emergence of right-wing governments and the proliferation of violence against minority groups (Bergmann, Kenney and Sutton 2018). Mapping projects such as the Southern Poverty Law Center's Hate Map, which tracks hate groups in the US; and Torn Apart/Separados, which tracks the implications of US immigration policies, are examples of other projects that have emerged in response to the climate of violence (Hate Map n.d.; Ahmed et al. 2018). These different projects serve as important reference points for our work on Intolerance Tracker.

In the following sections of this chapter, we examine the means and challenges of gathering data, the visual aspects of mapping and the challenges of dissemination and advocacy.

The Means and Challenges of Gathering Data

The proliferation of many hate-mapping websites in the context of India's and South Asia's rising intolerance reflected an urgent need to document incidents as they occur in order to archive the data and also employ them for advocacy. A key debate, when initial discussions on Intolerance Tracker started, was on the means of data collection, and how incidents of intolerance would be mapped on the platform. Our initial focus was on publicising the website and crowdsourcing the data; however, ultimately the website was populated by a small team of volunteers who worked with Intolerance Tracker and at other one-off events such as hackathons and workshops. In each instance, questions of data neutrality and political bias were central to our discussions, which was linked with the wider debates about the very concept of intolerance itself.

A key concern was about how to deal with bias in mapping the data. From the perspective of scientific methodology alone, using crowdsourcing as a means of producing digital data (whether in maps or other visual forms) came up quickly against allegations of bias (Eickhoff 2018; Tsou 2015). But as more reflective accounts of crowdmapping and crowdsourcing show, the idea of a lack of bias in other forms of map-making is a fallacy—if anything, online mapping is better able to make its 'biases' visible (Quattrone et al. 2015). Classical cartography itself was full of biases and ambiguities hidden under its seemingly authoritative, singular representation of spatial data (Harley 1987). Similar concerns of self-selection and bias arose when the primary means of building maps became volunteer-driven. Just as crowdsourcing reflects a certain participation bias, would not similar biases operate in our team?

In light of this, we decided early on that bias could not be prevented, but it was important to identify and make clear our intentions with Intolerance Tracker, and that it reflected a specific worldview, one that sided with minorities and the powerless. To begin with, this was done by deciding on a definition of intolerance that suited a broad range of acts of intolerance (and not restricting ourselves to overt physical violence) and looking at intolerance as a systematic progression, rather than a one-off event. Two guiding principles were behind this definition: the 1981 declaration by the UN General Assembly (OHCHR 1981) on the elimination of all forms of intolerance and discrimination based on religion or belief and the 1995 UNESCO Declaration of the Principles of Tolerance that sees tolerance as a rejection of 'dogmatism and absolutism' and 'an active attitude prompted by recognition of the universal human rights and fundamental freedoms of others' (UNESCO 1995; deSouza, Sharma and Rehman 2016). These cover a broad variety of incidents—from hate speech to terrorist violence.

In addition to seeking a broad and progressive definition of intolerance, we also identified key axes of exclusion and discrimination across South Asia, along which we would then map incidents of hate and intolerance. These included caste, ethnicity, religion, gender, sexuality and advocating for these groups or dissenting against the government, which in more recent times came increasingly under fire. Perpetrators, similarly, included not just individuals, or social and political groups, but also actors of the state, such as police or other government bodies. Including the state as an agent that promotes and even incites intolerance (even where it was carried out by other actors), threw into sharp relief the need for tacit or overt state support to perpetuate these agendas. In 2016, for instance, when we began mapping, we found that in an overwhelming number of cases involving the state (86), a majority of cases (64) involved instances where dissent or criticism of the state was being smothered (as in the case of the JNU incident mentioned earlier). In India—a country otherwise seen as the world's largest democracy—colonial-era sedition laws are particularly being used repeatedly to stifle dissent (Livemint 2019). The map was a way to document and reflect on these instances.

Our model of collecting data was to source stories of intolerance (based on our definition) across South Asia from reputable newspapers and news websites. Once again, this has the potential for introducing further forms of bias. To start with, who decides what is reputable? In most instances, this meant that we relied on mainstream news outlets (either online or print) to report incidents of intolerance, citing the links or images of newspapers alongside summaries of the incidents, and then adding relevant tags (whether incidents are caste- or gender-related and/or whether perpetrators are individuals or groups). While this might seemingly open us up to critiques of neutrality, it is important to point out here that just as with maps there is no such thing as pure 'objectivity' in news reporting even in mainstream media (This is well studied but some recent publications from a variety of disciplines are: Aaldering and Van der Pas 2018; Adegbola et al. 2018; Kearns et al. 2019). Recent approaches to journalism are more self-aware about pretences to objectivity, and instead embrace subjectivity and bias as a tool of reporting, rather than attempting to obscure it under the guise of neutrality (Chong 2019). Equally, given the recent proliferation of 'fake news', especially from the right-wing, the reliance on a largely fixed set of mainstream media outlets, while an imperfect solution, was the best possible one.

That said, mainstream media's bias itself had the tendency to be reflected on the map. Certain regions—for instance, Northeast India—tended to be underrepresented in light of their general neglect in mainstream Indian or South Asian media (Kikon 2009). As a result, the map disproportionately came to reflect the region as not being particularly affected, even though in reality it is often the site of violence and conflict, and the site of some of the most brutal state-led oppression in the country (deSouza, Sharma and Rehman 2016; Bhawsar et al. 2017). More problematically, news outlets are themselves frequently subject to violence and silencing from the state as well as non-state forces. This was most recently demonstrated in Pakistan where journalists and media organisations were subjected to crackdowns, censorship and even arrests and kidnappings (Tanzeem 2018; Hanif 2018). Moreover, by reporting incidents that appear in the news (which are deemed newsworthy by the outlets that report them), the map privileges the visibility of more extreme events over the structural, everyday forms of intolerance that enable the existence of larger events. Our method of data collection (relying on news outlets) did limit the portrayal of structural and systematic events, but in adopting a broader definition of intolerance (that is, beyond just physical violence) we hope to address this issue somewhat. What was and remains most important to our team is, at the bare minimum, to document and archive what was already publicly available—to not allow it to remain only as fragments of information but to show the larger patterns of oppression, and string them together in a visual narrative. Moving forward, we remain attentive to the many ways in which our reliance on sourcing data through mainstream media sources might inadvertently extend or reify the symptoms (particularly the silencing or neglect of certain voices, groups and areas) of some of the very forces that we are trying to address and counter (Bhawsar et al. 2017). We recognise that these are challenges, and going forward we aim to address some of these issues through future partnerships with researchers, journalists, community organisations and NGOs. We believe that this will allow for a more diverse range of sources and a richer and deeper engagement with the landscapes of intolerance.

The Visual Aspects of Mapping

Representing discrete incidents of violence and intolerance within a particular visual and (carto)graphic format raised further questions about neutrality and legibility, as well as the implications of representing processes across a region prominently marked by a long history of cartographic violence. As discussed above, we were interested in visually linking stories that would otherwise seem spatially and temporally distant from each other, separated by ideological and political divisions ingrained in and maintained by the highly militarised national borders of South Asian states. Yet South Asia's shared histories, cultures and politics mean that, despite the political rhetoric emphasising differences, incidents between different countries often share similar characteristics, and forms of violence can find chilling echoes across borders ('honour' killings in India and Pakistan are one such example). By using colour-coded categories to sort the types of incidents (for instance caste-, gender- and religion-motivated violence) and types of perpetrators, we aimed to make legible the connections as well as the underlying structures, trends and patterns.

While the use of these categories provided an initial tool of analysis to cut the data across different trends of intolerance, we also became aware of the limitations of singular categories. By placing each incident into a particular type of 'box', we were also potentially restricting a view that emphasised the intersections between different forms of violence. For instance, the analysis of cases of forced conversion of Hindu women in Pakistan has revealed a complicated landscape of overlapping patriarchal and political, rather than simply religious or proselytising, factors at play within particular contexts (Schaflechner 2018).

An early decision about visualising incidences of intolerance was to combine a spatial and temporal view of these events. Mapping discrete events on a map, tagged according to their categories, would highlight hotspots and spatial patterns of intolerance and violence (albeit skewed somewhat by media emphasis as discussed earlier) and help aggregate individual instances within the wider regional landscape to emphasise the geographic scale of the issues. At the same time, a timeline would enable us to capture their continuities (and discontinuities) and to help draw linkages through a narrative structure. We thus turned to Timescape, an online mapping platform explicitly designed to foreground the 'storytelling' potential of cartographic practices by incorporating a timeline as part of the main interface. Each incident mapped could then be treated as a story, or perhaps, as we started to think about it, as one part of an unfolding story—a meta-narrative as well as an archive of regional intolerance. As one scrolled down and clicked on stories on the timeline on the left-hand side of the screen, they would be simultaneously highlighted and popped up on the map, indicating the spatial structure of these wider unfolding stories. The spatio-temporal emphasis of Timescape's visual architecture, thus, allowed us to conceive of Intolerance Tracker as a way of 'leaving cartographic traces, making these (individual) experiences more visible and more tangible' (Caquard and Cartwright 2014).

Another early concern was about the political implications of a particular geographic view of the region that these stories would be aggregated on. Timescape was itself built using Google Maps and satellite image as base maps. As Weber, Temper and Del Bene discuss in detail in this book, Google Maps and similar platforms—despite, or perhaps because of, their technical and functional ubiquity—can present a range of tensions when used in conjunction with projects otherwise premised on emancipatory and progressive agendas. Crucially, they can reify and naturalise boundaries and hegemonic delineations of territories while obscuring a myriad of contestations and claims. As Intolerance Tracker came online, we were immediately attuned to these concerns. From the messy and ambiguous demarcations during decolonisation to current day disputes, South Asia's border regions—from Kashmir to Bengal—are not only the sites for chauvinistic proclamations of state sovereignty and nationalism but also contingent zones of negotiation and subversion where these proclamations are negotiated and complicated on a daily basis (see, for instance, Leake and Haines 2017; Chatterji 1999). We recognised the challenges of reconciling the universalised and naturalising views of the Google base map with the attention to local conditions and contingency that we sought from the project. While the use of alternative maps was technically out of the scope of our current resources, we addressed the issue, albeit partially, by switching Intolerance Tracker's default view to the satellite image, which we hoped would de-emphasise divisive state boundaries in favour of a picture of a more sutured regional topography.

Advocacy and Dissemination of the Platform

From the visual presentation, another key element of crowdmapping is the idea of the community. Building advocacy and community around the map has been challenging because, not only does Intolerance Tracker exist in a time of information overload with multiple social media platforms, it also exists in an era of disinformation.

In January 2019, WhatsApp announced that it would limit the number of times that its users could forward content to only five (Indian Express Tech Desk 2019). This was executed in response to the growing misinformation across India on its platform, a consequence that galvanised lynch mobs destroying communities and lives (Dixit and Mac 2018; McLaughlin 2018). This kind of mob violence provoked by information on social media was not unique to India, the Sri Lankan government in 2018 had to shut down social media platforms including WhatsApp and Facebook temporarily because these platforms were being used to incite violence against the Muslim minority (Kozlowska 2018).

The speed and volume with which information is shared on WhatsApp are such that there is neither enough time to engage constructively with it nor to verify or critically examine the data. As a result, just by sheer reach and repeated sharing, stories gain a degree of authenticity, which is then hard to question or rebut. With its scope and reach, and the certainty with which users propound information, WhatsApp has been wryly described as India's leading university (Roy 2018).

While Intolerance Tracker was launched before this unabashed bravado in using disinformation to further political gains it is very much located in a cycle of political, religious and ethnic violence that has been influenced and in parts impacted by social media and the twenty-four hours news cycle. One of the ambitions of Intolerance Tracker as a platform was to ensure that amidst the huge volumes of information, incidents of intolerance, however minor, would not be lost or subsumed in a stream of other news (deSouza and Sharma 2016).

The goals of our advocacy outreach were three-pronged. First, it was to ensure that the platform would provide a space to *acknowledge* that there were instances of violence, whether micro or macro aggressions, across South Asia, particularly in the countries that we studied. It was important to ensure that these incidents were 'named'—whether a fight at a food festival or a killing over possession of beef—to raise awareness about their occurrences. Second, it was important to *document* instances of intolerance and to ensure that they were remembered along with those that garnered greater public attention. The act of remembering—even petty crimes or thefts that had religious or ethnic influences—was essential because they helped to demonstrate how insidious violence had become across particular spaces in these countries. Third, it was to *analyse* how different incidents co-related and how these many incidents emerged in the context in which they appeared (see Figure 5.2). Were they instances of systemic violence, were they marginal infractions, what was the deeper underlying impact of all these different episodes? These were all aspects that we sought to investigate.

As a platform, therefore, Intolerance Tracker primarily sought to be a database, one that could, through media reported narratives, acknowledge, document and analyse different episodes of violence. From this, it was envisaged that through the database, which has about 700 incidents, attempts could be made by reporters, activists, governments and academics to understand why incidents of violence emerged across particular geographies and times.

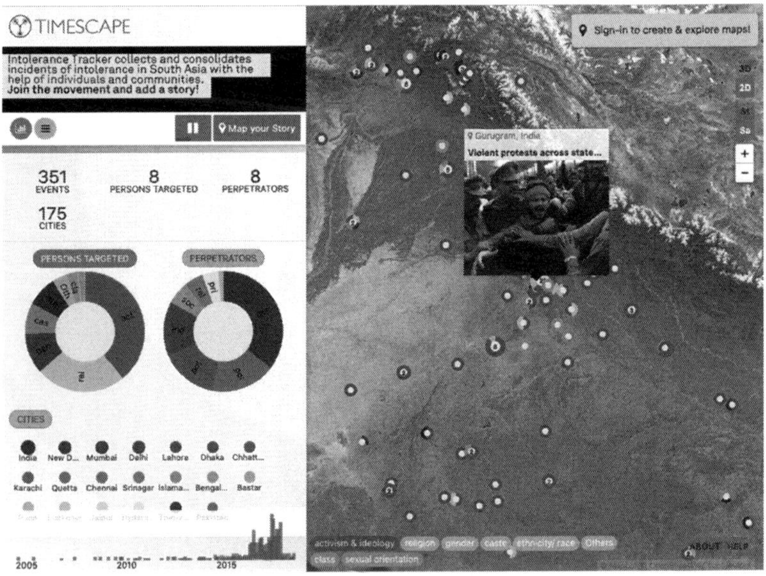

Figure 5.2: Data analytics on Intolerance Tracker.
Source: Intolerance Tracker website.

In addition to being a database for research, one of our ambitions with the platform was for it to be a *monitoring* device, an aid to help those who wished to speak truth to power. In the past three years of running the platform, the sheer breadth of incidents that have now become normalised highlights the need to have space where they continue to be called out for what they are. For example, in the past three years, the question of food has become a major point of conflict in India, resulting in the deaths of many people. Restaurants are now celebrating India–Pakistan tensions by offering 'surgical strikes' discounts on their meals (Gauba 2016). In India, some consider speaking out against the government means you are an 'anti-national' and asked to leave the country for Pakistan (Bureau 2016). All these examples that should have been roundly criticised are now part of the mainstream vocabulary. The idea of this reservoir of data from where civil society can monitor the actions of governments was meant to ensure that in an era of fake news, where media houses regularly abridge and delete news reports, there would be an independent database to call governments out. In this way, the platform aims to be a device that arms activists with information to counter dominant narratives that seek to downplay these incidents.

A long term ambition of the platform is for it to be a data resource from where judicial and legislative actions could be taken. However, for this, the platform requires to have a critical mass in order to have any meaningful impact, a challenge that we are working towards.

We have tried to adopt different approaches to build an outreach, which includes using Facebook and Twitter to highlight stories that are already reported on the platform. In addition to sharing stories, we have ran online campaigns that highlighted a particular issue a month, and have also organised an online mapathon. These campaigns garnered some support, but, in general, we were unable to convince people to use the platform to document stories. Much of our advocacy efforts have not reached the scale that could influence public discourse, and as a result, while we aspire to be a crowdsourced platform as mentioned earlier, the platform is primarily run by a small team of volunteers. One of the reasons, we think, is that there are too many social media platforms out there, which could potentially cause fatigue among users to try another platform. Additionally, we also think that, because our social media followers are limited, we are not able to get the word out to enough people, as the platform's algorithms are designed to correspond to the size of its followers.

One of our more successful outreach programs was going to universities and conducting in-person workshops on the use of Intolerance Tracker as a platform for research and advocacy. In workshops in Delhi and Berlin, we worked with students to collect and report stories through guided mapping sessions around particular themes of intolerance. These in-person sessions, along with a series of opinion pieces that we wrote for news outlets such as openDemocracy, Kafila and The Conversation, were crucial in bringing different users to the platform.

We often remarked that Intolerance Tracker has remained completely under the radar, and the evidence for this has been borne by the fact that, in an age of trolling, our platform was trolled only once. This was in direct contrast to the 'Hate Tracker' project of the *Hindustan Times* in India mentioned earlier, which closed down abruptly, soon after a publicity blitz on its launch (The Wire Staff 2017). The *Hindustan Times*'s Hate Tracker, in its short time of operation, had, however, managed to attract several eyeballs through a series of smart social media marketing plugs using infographics and video blurbs. Its demise is illustrative of the relevance and importance of such a project in the current times. The other projects such as Halt the Hate and HateHatao have used a combination of opinion-based articles in mainstream media and social media outreach through Twitter, Facebook and YouTube to build more traction around their projects.

The challenge for Intolerance Tracker is to convey to different audiences why it is important to collaboratively build such databases, and why the data from such platforms can have a far-reaching impact.

Conclusion

As we enter the third year of running the platform, Intolerance Tracker aims to focus on updating and building its database through collaborations and partnerships. Given the wealth of projects out there, there are many opportunities to find synergies and pool resources. We hope that in the years ahead, the database will begin to reflect stories not just from mainstream media in South Asia, but also from the vernacular press; and that its users will come not just from big cities, but also from smaller towns. In time, we hope to build a multi-lingual platform that can be used by people across South Asia, and we hope to reduce the entry barriers by introducing new tech-based solutions to get inputs from the larger public.

As South Asia continues to witness horrific violence against minorities and other vulnerable groups, we believe that platforms such as Intolerance Tracker need to persist to ensure that stories of violence and hate are not normalised.

References

Aaldering, L. and Daphne van der Pas. 'Political Leadership in the Media: Gender Bias in Leader Stereotypes During Campaign and Routine Times'. *British Journal of Political Science* (2018): 1–21. DOI: 10.1017/S0007123417000795.

Adegbola, O., J. Skarda-Mitchell and S. Gearhart. 'Everything's Negative About Nigeria: A Study of US Media Reporting on Nigeria'. *Global Media and Communication* 14, no. 1 (2018): 47–63.

Ahmed, Manan, Maira E. Álvarez, Sylvia A. Fernández, Alex Gil, Merisa Martinez, Moacir P. de Sá Pereira, Linda Rodriguez and Roopika Risam. 2018. 'Torn Apart/Separados'. 25 June 2018. http://xpmethod.plaintext.in/torn-apart/volume/2/index (accessed on 12 January 2020).

'Avijit Roy'. *PEN America* (blog). 6 July 2016. https://pen.org/advocacy-case/avijit-roy/ (accessed on 12 January 2020).

BBC Staff. 'Karachi Ismailis Massacred on Bus'. Asia. *BBC*. 13 May 2015. https://www.bbc. com/news/world-asia-32717321 (accessed on 12 January 2020).

Bergmann, Max, Carolyn Kenney and Trevor Sutton. 'The Rise of Far-Right Populism Threatens Global Democracy and Security'. Center for American Progress. 2 November 2018. https://www.americanprogress.org/issues/security/news/2018/11/02/460498/rise-far-right-populism-threatens-global-democracy-security/ (accessed on 12 January 2020).

Bhawsar, Vaibhav, Siddharth Peter de Souza, Nida Rehman, Somnath Ray and Saba Sharma. 'Geographies of Racism, Fascism and Intolerance: Mapping Hate, Recording Violence'. openDemocracy. 17 May 2017. https://www.opendemocracy.net/en/geographies-of-racism-fascism-and-intolerance-mapping-hate-recording-violence/ (accessed on 12 January 2020).

Biswas, Soutik. 'Five India "sedition" Students Return to JNU'. India. *BBC*, 22 February 2016. https://www.bbc.com/news/world-asia-india-35628170 (accessed on 12 January 2020).

Boone, Jon. 'Sabeen Mahmud, Pakistani Rights Activist, Shot Dead'. World News. *The Guardian*, 25 April 2015. https://www.theguardian.com/world/2015/apr/25/sabeen-mehmud-pakistani-womens-rights-activist-shot-dead (accessed on 12 January 2020).

Bureau, Our. 'Rahul Is Anti-National, Should Go to Pakistan: BJP'. *News Businessline*, 19 February 2016. https://www.thehindubusinessline.com/news/rahul-is-antinational-should-go-to-pakistan-bjp/article8258284.ece (accessed on 12 January 2020).

Burke, Jason and Agencies. 'Protests to Continue at Indian University after Student Leader's Arrest'. World News. *The Guardian*, 15 February 2016. https://www.theguardian.com/world/2016/feb/15/jawaharlal-nehru-university-kanhaiya-kumar-student-arrest-india. (accessed on 12 January 2020).

Caquard, Sébastien and William Cartwright. 'Narrative Cartography: From Mapping Stories to the Narrative of Maps and Mapping'. *The Cartographic Journal* 51, no. 2 (2014): 101–106. https://doi.org/10.1179/0008704114Z.000000000130 (accessed on 12 January 2020).

Chaney, Paul and Sarbeswar Sahoo. 'Civil society and the contemporary threat to religious freedom in Bangladesh'. *Journal of Civil Society* 16, no. 3 (2020): 191–215.

Chatterji, Joya. 'The Fashioning of a Frontier: The Radcliffe Line and Bengal's Border Landscape, 1947–52'. *Modern Asian Studies* 33, no. 1 (1999): 185–242.

Chong, P. 'Valuing Subjectivity in Journalism: Bias, Emotions, and Self-interest as Tools in Arts Reporting'. *Journalism* 20, no. 3 (2019): 427–443.

De Souza, Siddharth Peter and Saba Sharma. 'Intolerance Tracker–A Community Curated Visual Storytelling Platform'. Kafila—12 Years of a Common Journey (blog). 2 March 2016. https://kafila.online/2016/03/02/intolerance-tracker-a-community-curated-visual-storytelling-platform-siddharth-peter-de-souza-and-saba-sharma/ (accessed on 12 January 2020).

De Souza, Siddharth Peter, Saba Sharma and Nida Rehman. 'What We've Found by Mapping Incidents of Intolerance Across South Asia'. *The Conversation*, 2016. http://theconversation.com/what-weve-found-by-mapping-incidents-of-intolerance-across-south-asia-66181 (accessed on 12 January 2020).

Dixit, Pranav and Ryan Mac. 'Vicious Rumors Spread Like Wildfire On WhatsApp—And Destroyed A Village'. *BuzzFeed News*, 2018. https://www.buzzfeednews.com/article/pranavdixit/whatsapp-destroyed-village-lynchings-rainpada-india (accessed on 12 January 2020).

Eickhoff, C. 'Cognitive Biases in Crowdsourcing'. Proceedings of the Eleventh ACM International Conference on Web Search and Data Mining—WSDM, 2018, 162–170.

Gauba, Prerna. 2016. 'Food Chain Offers Discount Over "Surgical Strike", Withdraws It After Criticism'. *Hindustan Times*, 30 September 2016. https://www.hindustantimes.com/india-news/food-chain-offers-discount-over-surgical-strike-withdraws-it-after-criticism/story-aYzbAWLU4D4seny5IYW8xH.html (accessed on 12 January 2020).

Halt the Hate. n.d. http://haltthehate.amnesty.org.in/ (accessed on 28 April 2019).

Hate Map. n.d. Southern Poverty Law Center. Accessed 28 April 2019. https://www.splcenter.org/hate-map (accessed on 12 January 2020).

Human Rights Watch. 'Violent Cow Protection in India: Vigilante Groups Attack Minorities'. *Human Rights Watch*, 18 February 2019. https://www.hrw.org/report/2019/02/18/violent-cow-protection-india/vigilante-groups-attack-minorities (accessed on 12 January 2020).

Indian Express Tech Desk. 'WhatsApp Forwards Restricted to Just Five Chats, Globally: Here's What It Means'. *Indian Express*, 2019. https://indianexpress.com/article/technology/social/whatsapp-restricting-forwards-to-just-five-chats-globally-5548492/ (accessed on 12 January 2020).

Kayani, Amir. 'Ahmadi Place of Worship Set Ablaze in Jhelum, Riots Erupt after Blasphemy Allegations—Pakistan'. *Dawn*. 21 November 2015. https://www.dawn.com/news/1221273 (accessed on 12 January 2020).

Kearns, E.M., A.E. Betus and A.F. Lemieux. 'Why Do Some Terrorist Attacks Receive More Media Attention Than Others?' *Justice Quarterly* 36, no. 6 (2019): 985–1022.

Kikon, D. 'The Predicament of Justice: Fifty Years of Armed Forces Special Powers Act in India'. *Contemporary South Asia* 17, no. 3(2009): 271–282.

Kozlowska, Hanna. 'Sri Lanka Shut Down Facebook, WhatsApp, and Instagram to Stop Anti-Muslim Violence'. *Quartz*, 2018. https://qz.com/1223787/sri-lanka-shut-down-facebook-whatsapp-and-instagram-to-stop-anti-muslim-violence/ (accessed on 12 January 2020).

Leake, Elisabeth and Daniel Haines. 'Lines of (In)Convenience: Sovereignty and Border-Making in Postcolonial South Asia, 1947–1965'. *The Journal of Asian Studies* 76, no. 4 (2017): 963–85. https://doi.org/10.1017/S0021911817000808

Livemint. 'Why India's Sedition Law Needs to be Buried'. Opinio. Livemint. 19 January 2019. https://www.livemint.com/Opinion/IQ2o3mXhLJ8kIzlVrStpZK/Why-Indias-sedition-law-needs-to-be-buried.html (accessed on 12 January 2020).

Mander, Harsh. 2018. 'New Hate Crime Tracker in India Finds Victims Are Predominantly Muslims, Perpetrators Hindus'. Text. Scroll.In. 2018. https://scroll.in/article/901206/new-hate-crime-tracker-in-india-finds-victims-are-predominantly-muslims-perpetrators-hindus (accessed on 12 January 2020).

McCarthy, Julie. 'In India, Catholic Church Attacks Spark Fears Of Intimidation'. Culture. *NPR*. 3 February 2015. https://www.npr.org/sections/parallels/2015/02/03/383454982/in-india-catholic-church-attacks-spark-fears-of-intimidation (accessed on 12 January 2020).

McLaughlin, Timothy. 'How WhatsApp Fuels Fake News and Violence in India'. *Wired*. 12 December 2018. https://www.wired.com/story/how-whatsapp-fuels-fake-news-and-violence-in-india/ (accessed on 12 January 2020).

Nair, Neeti. 'Rising Religious Intolerance in South Asia'. *Current History* 117, no. 798 (2018): 148–150.

OHCHR 1981. 'Declaration on the Elimination of All Forms of Intolerance and of Discrimination Based on Religion or Belief'. *UNHRC*. https://www.ohchr.org/EN/ProfessionalInterest/Pages/ReligionOrBelief.aspx (accessed on 12 January 2020).

Pandit, Maya. 'The Rot in Maharashtra'. *Economic and Political Weekly* 50, no. 7 (June 2015): 7–8.

Quattrone, G., L. Capra and P. De Meo. 'There's No Such Thing as the Perfect Map: Quantifying Bias in Spatial Crowdsourcing Datasets'. Proceedings of the 18th ACM Conference on Computer Supported Cooperative Work & Social Computing—CSCW '15', 2015, 1021–1032.

Riaz, Waseem, Abbas Haider, Nadeem Haider, Imran Gabol, Agencies and Ali Akbar. '15 Killed in Taliban Attack on Lahore Churches'. News. Dawn. 15 March 2015. http://www.dawn.com/news/1169713 (accessed on 12 January 2020).

Rizwi, Uzair Hasan. 'The Rising Threat Against Shia Muslims in Pakistan'. Politics, *The Wire*. 11 June 2016. https://thewire.in/politics/the-rising-threat-against-shia-muslims-in-pakistan (accessed on 12 January 2020).

Sahu, Manish. 'Agra "Ghar Wapsi": A Year Later, Main Accused out on Bail as Cops Await Govt Prosecution Sanction'. *The Indian Express* (blog). 8 December 2015. https://indianexpress.com/article/cities/lucknow/agra-ghar-wapsi-a-year-later-main-accused-out-on-bail-as-cops-await-govt-prosecution-sanction/ (accessed on 12 January 2020).

Scroll Staff. 'MM Kalburgi Murder: Supreme Court Agrees to Hear Plea for SIT Inquiry on February 26'. Text. Scroll.In. 25 January 2019. https://scroll.in/latest/910823/mm-kalburgi-murder-supreme-court-agrees-to-hear-plea-for-sit-inquiry-on-february-26 (accessed on 12 January 2020).

Schaflechner, Jürgen. '"Forced Conversions" of Hindu Women to Islam in Pakistan: Another Perspective'. The Conversation. Accessed 22 March 2020. http://theconversation.com/forced-conversions-of-hindu-women-to-islam-in-pakistan-another-perspective-102726 (accessed on 12 January 2020).

Setalvad, Teesta. 'HateHatao, a Revolutionary New App Designed to Fight Hate Speech'. Rights. *The Wire*. 30 January 2019. https://thewire.in/rights/hate-hatao-app-cjp (accessed on 12 January 2020).

Shroff. 'Three Years On, Remember the "Dadri Lynching"'. Amnesty International India. 28 September 2018. https://amnesty.org.in/three-years-on-remember-the-dadri-lynching/ (accessed on 12 January 2020).

Tharoor, Ishaan. 'These Bangladeshi Bloggers Were Murdered by Islamist Extremists. Here Are Some of Their Writings'. Worldviews. *Washington Post*. 2016. https://www.washingtonpost.com/news/worldviews/wp/2016/04/29/these-bangladeshi-bloggers-were-murdered-by-islamist-extremists-here-are-some-of-their-writings/ (accessed on 12 January 2020).

Tsou, M.H. 'Research Challenges and Opportunities in Mapping Social Media and Big Data'. *Cartography and Geographic Information Science* 42, sup. 1 (2015): 70–74.

The Wire Staff. 2016. 'Standing With JNU, from Around the World – Statements of Solidarity'. *The Wire*. 2016. https://thewire.in/government/standing-with-jnu-from-around-the-world-statements-of-solidarity (accessed on 12 January 2020).

The Wire Staff. 'After Editor's Exit, Hindustan Times Pulls Down Controversial "Hate Tracker"'. *The Wire*. 2017. https://thewire.in/media/hindustan-times-hate-tracker (accessed on 12 January 2020).

———. 'Real or Fake, We Can Make Any Message Go Viral: Amit Shah to BJP Social Media Volunteers'. *The Wire*. 2018. https://thewire.in/politics/amit-shah-bjp-fake-social-media-messages (accessed on 12 January 2020).

UNESCO 1995. 'Declaration of Principles on Tolerance'. http://portal.unesco.org/en/ev.php-URL_ID=13175&URL_DO=DO_TOPIC&URL_SECTION=201.html (accessed on 12 January 2020).

'Xulhaz Mannan'. *PEN America* (blog). 30 June 2016. https://pen.org/advocacy-case/xulhaz-mannan/ (accessed on 12 January 2020).

6

ADVANCING A FACTUAL, RIGHTS-BASED NARRATIVE OF PALESTINE AND PALESTINIANS (PALESTINE OPEN MAPS)

Interview with Ahmad Barclay, by Siddharth Peter de Souza

Can you tell us a little about Palestine Open Maps and what your role in the project is?

Palestine Open Maps (POM)—palopenmaps.org—is an online platform developed by Visualizing Palestine (VP) for digitising, navigating, searching and downloading historic and present-day maps of Palestine/ Israel.

Launched in 2012 as the first project of Visualizing Impact, VP seeks to harness data-driven visual media—including infographics, animations and interactive experiences—to advance a factual, rights-based narrative on Palestine and Palestinians. The VP team includes researchers, designers, developers and storytellers working across Western Asia, North Africa, Europe and North America.

POM was initiated by VP in early 2018, and I have led the work on the project up to now.

How did the project idea emerge and what were the main objectives? Please tell us about particular experiences or encounters that shaped these ideas.

The idea for the project emerged after we discovered that a large number of highly detailed British Mandate maps of Palestine from the 1930s and 1940s had been made available, along with many other maps, via an online viewer on the website of the National Library of Israel. Through this platform, the individual map sheets could be viewed, but could not be meaningfully navigated, searched or downloaded.

Comprising more than 150 sheets, the maps contain an amazing wealth of information, naming tens of thousands of points of interest—towns, villages, mountains, rivers, valleys, religious sites, railway stations, water cisterns, mills, threshing floors—as they existed immediately before the Nakba (the forcible displacement of over 750,000 Palestinians in 1947–49 from their homes in the area that became Israel).

It is hard to overstate the historical, political and cultural importance of these maps since many of the locations that they feature have since been destroyed, renamed or otherwise erased from official Israeli maps. Their power is captured vividly by the Israeli political scientist Meron Benvenisti in his book *Sacred Landscape: The Buried History of the Holy Land Since 1948*, as it describes his efforts to uncover an erased Palestinian history:

> I couldn't have done anything without the marvelous detailed maps (scale 1:20,000) compiled by the Mandatory authorities and updated just before the 1948 War. I would spread the relevant map on the ground, and suddenly the old landscape arose like an apparition: village houses, mosques, school buildings, paths, stone hedges marking plot boundaries, limekilns, threshing floors, holy tombs, sacred oak trees, springs and cisterns, caves, fruit trees, patches of cultivation. And each plot and every prominent feature had its Arabic name marked on the map, so poetic and so apt [...] that my heart ached (Benvenisti 2000).

The driving aim of the project for us was to 'open source' these maps. They were already in the public domain—and, therefore, free of copyright or other usage restrictions—but we wanted to make them accessible and usable to real people, from third and fourth generation Palestinian refugees to geographers, historians, educators and political activists.

How did you and your team plan to build upon the initial ideas? We would love to hear about the process of building the site. Were there any particular models or comparable projects that drove the thinking?
We had a chance to develop the initial idea for the platform during a March 2018 workshop that Visualizing Impact, VP's parent organisation, co-organised with Columbia University's Studio-X Amman, in Amman, Jordan. Over the course of three intensive days of work, we managed to put together a basic 'proof of concept' prototype that allowed users to navigate through a selection of the maps that we had collected, and to access basic information on towns and villages,

past and present. Based on this, within around a month, we built a usable version of the platform for public alpha launch.

The team that worked on the project at this stage included a GIS and data management systems specialist, a back-end and a front-end web developer and myself, as an architecturally trained information designer.

One project that has inspired us has been the US Geological Survey's TopoView, a service that allows users to navigate and download over 100,000 maps of the United States at various scales and different points in history. Another has been the New York Public Library Space/Time project, which engages the general public in curating historical and geographic information on the city through a series of easy to use tools.

Tell us about the decision to work with a map-based interface, as well as any design considerations and outcomes. Were there particular objectives or challenges in terms of how you made these representations?

To the VP team, a Google Maps-style 'slippy map' interface was the most familiar and intuitive way to make the maps accessible to almost any web user. Our number one aim was to make the maps as easily accessible as possible, and this type of interface is something familiar and intuitive to almost any web user and allows for the possibility to pan and zoom through huge maps on a screen as small as a smartphone. We also implemented a basic search functionality to find towns and villages by name, though we would like to develop this much further to eventually locate any kind of place of interest contained within the maps (see Figure 6.1).

One decision that we made early in the process was to translate the maps from the 'Palestine 1923 Grid' to the 'Web Mercator' projection, which is used by virtually all major web mapping platforms, including Google Maps, Bing Maps, OpenStreetMap and Mapbox, making it easy to combine and overlay the historic maps with readily available layers such as present-day aerial photography.

What were the primary data sources and the challenges in working with them?

The first challenge for us was to actually download the maps. They could be viewed online in high resolution, but could not easily be downloaded for use in other ways. In the end, we developed a series of scripts that allowed us to automate the process of downloading (or 'scraping') the maps from the website in small chunks, and to piece them back together to recreate the full resolution map sheets.

The next challenge was to combine the maps into web map layers, which involved cropping, georeferencing, colour correcting and merging hundreds of map sheets, converting these to the Web Mercator projection, and then creating the 'tilesets' for viewing online (mosaics of tens of thousands of image tiles that are loaded through the web browser). We did almost all of this work with open source tools, including QGIS.

Another significant ongoing challenge for us has been in compiling the names, geographic coordinates and other information for all of the towns and villages in both the present day and prior to 1948. We relied on a number of different sources, including Israeli and Palestinian government data, Salman Abu Sitta's *Atlas of Palestine* and the NGO Zochrot, as well as the 1945 'Village Statistics' compiled by British Mandate authorities. We found many discrepancies between the different datasets and the maps themselves, and the process of combining them was painstaking.

As an open-source map, how did you build a community around the project? How have you sustained their interest in the project?

Firstly, it's important to note that Visualizing Palestine has built a large community of subscribers and members since we began our work in 2012 and that this community itself is part of a wider global movement supporting Palestinian rights and, more often than not, other social justice causes. So, when we launched the Palestine Open Maps project in May 2018, we already had a receptive audience that was ready to engage with it and was already used to using and sharing our content, which is invariably shared under a Creative Commons license.

Another community-building aspect unique to Palestine Open Maps has been 'mapathon' events, organised by Majd Al-shihabi, the lead developer on the project. The aim of the mapathons has been to bring together volunteers to digitise (or 'vectorise') all of the geographic information contained within the historic maps, but it has proven to be a powerful way to actively engage people in using and sharing the platform in general. To date, we have organised mapathons in Beirut, Amman, London, Cambridge, Milan and in Burj Shemali and Beddawi refugee camps in Lebanon.

What kind of response has Palestine Open Maps received? Who are your audiences? Have other organisations or groups reached out to use/build on it in particular ways?

In the first week that the site was launched, we received over 10,000 unique visitors and had media write-ups in multiple languages, for example, English and Italian. Individuals have reached out to us from a number of institutions, including academics at Oxford University, who are making active use of the platform, and we have been invited to present the project at the Mozilla Festival and the Creative Commons Global Summit. We also will be planning a mapathon event with the British Library in London.

Another collaboration that we are excited about is working with the Palestinian Oral History Archive (POHA) at the American University of Beirut to create an interactive map to navigate the interviews in their database using hundreds of landmarks that can be found on the maps. POHA includes more than 1,000 hours of testimonies with first-generation Palestinian refugees forcibly displaced in the Nakba, which make reference to over 800 landmarks, from mountains, valleys and rivers to schools, cinemas and holy sites.

What was the most challenging aspect—practical or conceptual—of building and working with Palestine Open Maps?

The major challenge for the project right now is to build on the momentum of its first year to create something sustainable in the long term, both in terms of funding and organisation. So far we have been supported primarily through Visualizing Impact core funding, the entity through which Visualizing Palestine operates, with Majd's work being supported by the Bassel Khartabil Free Culture Fellowship (funded by Creative Commons, Wikimedia and other organisations) and others working as volunteers.

In the coming months, we are aiming to find grants, fellowships and other sources of funding to allow us to build towards the bigger vision that we have for the project, as well as to structure the team and governance of the project in the most effective way.

What are your objectives with respect to advocacy and outreach? What kind of tools do you use and how do you see its impact being maximised?

Our primary objective through the project is for the maps to be seen and used by as many people as possible. We believe that the sheer existence and visibility of these maps challenge the active erasure of Palestine from official maps over the past seventy years.

Besides sharing the platform through Visualizing Palestine's community, the mapathon events are proving to be an effective way to build a whole new community to disseminate and actively contribute to the project (see Figure 6.3). Participating in the digitisation process, which involves tracing and naming the individual features of the maps at an intimate level of detail, offers an entirely different level of perspective and engagement compared to just viewing the maps as an observer.

What are the goals for Palestine Open Maps and the team going forward?

Besides the aim of making the project sustainable and continuing the process of digitising the maps, we also have a number of projects and ideas for how the digital platform can extend into the physical world.

As Visualizing Palestine, we have already created and exhibited 3-dimensional art pieces based on the historic maps together with installation artist Marwan Rechmaoui under the title 'A National Monument'. The work comprises of twenty-one topographic reliefs depicting the major Palestinian towns and cities before the Nakba (see Figure 6.2).

We are also discussing the possibility to create augmented reality experiences with the maps and to create a series of printed maps and atlases that could potentially be sold as a means to sustain the project financially.

Alongside all of these things, we also want to open-source the tools we are building, making them available to others who want to initiate similar projects in other parts of the world.

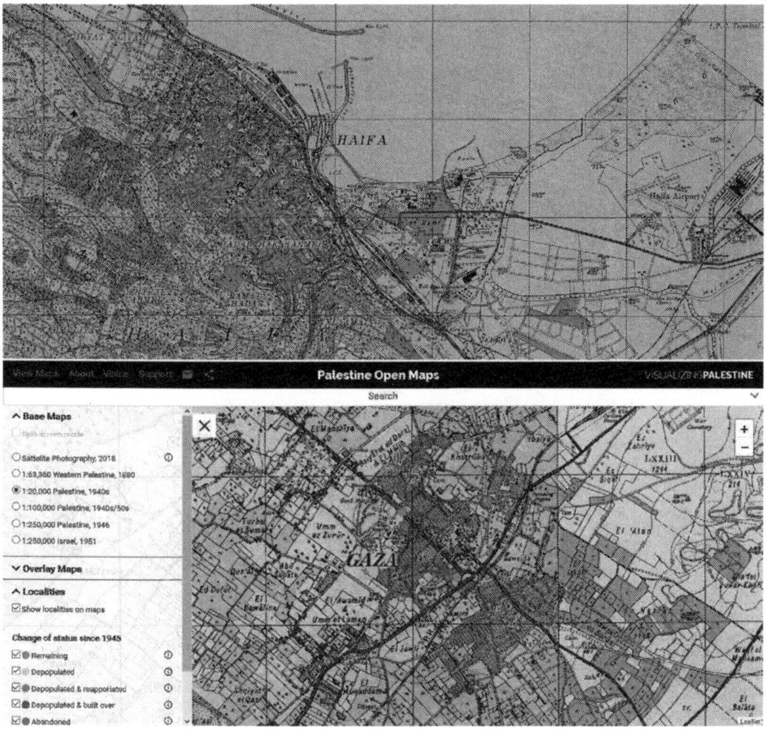

Figure 6.1: Detail of 1:20,000 scale Haifa map sheet, Survey of Palestine, 1942 (top). POM interface (bottom). *Source: Palestine Open Maps website.*

Figure 6.2: Milan mapathon, March 2019 (left) and Burj Shemali mapathon, November 2018 (right). Photos by OpenDot and Ahmad Barclay.

Figure 6.3: A National Monument, 3-dimensional artwork depicting 21 Palestinian cities before the Nakba (left). Close-up of Haifa piece from A National Monument (right). Photos by Joe Kairouz.

Reference

Benvenisti, Meron. *Sacred Landscape: The Buried History of the Holy Land Since 1948*, trans. Maxine Kaufman-Lacusta. Berkeley: University of California Press, 2000.

PART III

FEMINIST INTERVENTIONS

7

MAPPING AND STOPPING SEXUAL HARASSMENT WITH HarassMap

Rebecca Chiao, Farah Shash, Angie Abdelmonem and Noora Flinkman

Introduction

Sexual harassment has been a problem of Egyptian public space for a long time. Yet, since the issue has also been steeped in taboo and silence for decades, harassers have largely been allowed to harass with impunity and the harassed have been scared or discouraged to speak up about their experiences. Until 2005, the only visible discussions addressing sexual harassment (among other forms of sexual violence) occurred in online communities, or the so called shadow publics (Abdelmonem 2015). In 2008, the Egyptian Centre for Women's Rights (ECWRs) published its ground-breaking, and now widely cited, study showing that 98 per cent of foreign and 83 per cent of Egyptian women surveyed reported having experienced sexual harassment—shedding some light on the magnitude of the problem (Hassan et al. 2008). The study, along with others that have been published since, has helped make visible the scope of the sexual harassment problem, including its prevalence; age and class demographics of those harassed and to some extent those who harass; the forms of sexual harassment experienced; locations where sexual harassment occurred and more. However, activism centring specifically on sexual harassment in Egypt has been limited or short-lived. Although events in 2005 and the January 2011 revolution spurred mobilisation around the issue, challenges have persisted as to how best to address the problem and create real, long-lasting change. In this chapter, we will tell the story of HarassMap, one of the most prominent anti-sexual harassment initiatives in Egypt, and look at how we have used technology and crowdmapping tools together with community mobilisation to combat sexual harassment.

The Origins of a Movement: Sexual Harassment Activism in Egypt

'Black Wednesday' in May 2005, when 'thugs' sexually harassed and assaulted female activists protesting a constitutional referendum outside of the Press Syndicate offices in downtown Cairo, was one of the key events that spurred some of the first activism to address public sexual harassment in Egypt (El Mahdi 2010). A short-lived movement called 'The Street is Ours' emerged to combat politically motivated sexual violence targeting activist women and protesters. In September of the same year, volunteer interns working at the Egyptian Centre for Women's Rights (ECWRs) founded a program that would become known as 'Making Our Streets Safe for Everyone' (Rizzo et al. 2012). The volunteers' program began in response to their own experiences, many of which had happened while commuting to ECWR and had been ignored by bystanders. Unlike 'The Street is Ours', the volunteers focused on combating everyday forms of street sexual harassment. Despite an enthusiastic response from the public, then international relations director at ECWR, Rebecca Chiao, noted that ECWR did not officially support this work until mid-2007, given the highly sensitive nature of the issue.

Rebecca and a small group of ECWR volunteers and employees began by distributing surveys on university campuses, at cultural venues, businesses, factories, ECWR trainings and via email. These surveys were designed to begin a conversation on women's experiences of and responses to sexual harassment, which at the time was not openly discussed. From 2005 through 2006, ECWR received thousands of surveys and dozens of volunteers. Rebecca and the volunteers sought to open conversations, publicise and coordinate ideas to work on the problem of sexual harassment wherever possible, including in various local media outlets.

In October of 2006, during Eid al-Adha celebrations, a mass sexual harassment incident occurred in downtown Cairo, which generated widespread national and international media interest (BBC 2006). Scores of young men shut out of a movie theatre, which was airing a new film by the now infamous Egyptian director Sobky, began harassing and assaulting groups of women walking in the area. These incidents were caught on video via mobile phone and uploaded to YouTube. Well-known bloggers, including Sand Monkey, Wael Abbas and MaLek X, denounced the event, and new public conversations on sexual harassment began to emerge. At the suggestion of a blogger named Nermeen Edrees, Rebecca and Edrees organised a demonstration in response to the incident. The demonstration was well attended, but ECWR and other NGOs remained hesitant to work on the issue.

In mid-2007, funding for the volunteers' sexual harassment program was offered, which prompted ECWR to officially adopt it. This allowed them to hold a public event attended by over 1,000 people, hire Engy Ghozlan to manage the project and formally undertake efforts to systematically investigate the problem in Egypt. The funded project consisted of three programmatic pillars: public outreach, work in schools and advocacy. One result was the 2008 'Clouds in Egypt's Sky' report. ECWR's sexual harassment study was the first of its kind in the country, garnering widespread attention for defining the pervasiveness of Egypt's sexual harassment problem.

Throughout 2007 and 2008, momentum picked up around ECWR's sexual harassment program, with increasing media and public attention directed at the issue and several legal outcomes. This was exemplified and amplified by the first successful criminal case on sexual harassment brought by Noha Roushdy, a flatmate of an ECWR anti-harassment volunteer, in 2008. While walking with a friend in the street, Roushdy was grabbed and dragged by a man driving by (Daily News Egypt 2008; Ilahi 2008). Persisting through initial police resistance to file a case against the driver, Roushdy succeeded in seeing her harasser convicted.

Following the Roushdy case, most women's NGOs in Egypt began work on sexual harassment through advocacy for a new law. By the end of 2008, ECWR had increasingly directed its attention towards legal advocacy as well. This included researching laws and the legal environment for sexual harassment across the region, which culminated in a 2009 press conference and report on the subject. ECWR was one of the organisations that drafted new legislative proposals seeking to introduce a definition of and penalties for sexual harassment in the penal code, which at the time went ignored by parliament and the president's office (FIDH 2014). Lost within this growing policy-oriented emphasis was a focus on the public or community-level change. Despite its early progress, the sexual harassment program was losing the momentum that had been growing in prior years and public mobilisation was decreasing.

Towards the end of 2008, Justin Kiggins, a volunteer, contacted Rebecca to suggest customising a version of the free, anonymous crowdmapping platform Ushahidi[1] and linking it together with Frontline SMS to create an online tool to combat sexual harassment in a new and innovative way. The idea was that victims or witnesses could send anonymous online or SMS reports of sexual harassment incidents, which would then be displayed on an online map. Before this, Ushahidi crowdmaps had largely been deployed to address conflicts, crises and emergencies, including the 2010 Haiti earthquake and election corruption in Kenya (Goodchild and Glennon 2010; Kahl 2012; Hester et al. 2010). Egypt would represent the first attempt at using crowdmapping to challenge a longer-term social problem such as sexual harassment. Since about 97 per cent of Egyptians owned a mobile phone, this SMS and web-based reporting technology seemed like an opportunity to move away from advocacy and top-down strategies and re-engage the public in anti-harassment activism. Rebecca worked together with three other co-founders (Engy Ghozlan, Sawsan Gad and Amel Fahmy) and volunteers, forming a new initiative that they would call HarassMap.

HarassMap: Ending Social Acceptability of Sexual Harassment

At the time of HarassMap's launch in 2010, legal recourse for people who experienced sexual harassment was limited by several barriers. Victim-blaming and negative effects on reputation were powerful deterrents keeping many silent, and away from police stations. Moreover, the law required people to bring their harasser to a police station and to secure witnesses. Individuals reporting sexual harassment risked additional harassment from police and had to convince officers to allow them to submit a criminal report. While not denying that legal reform was needed, the co-founders believed that in a context in which existing laws were not enforced because sexual harassment was not seen as a crime, advocacy for a new law would have little impact on its own. Therefore, they decided to tackle what they believed to be the source of non-enforcemen—social acceptability. This idea also remains at the core of HarassMap's work today.

In fact, there are strong social roots and established history in Egypt for rejecting sexual harassment. We believe that bringing back social discouragement needs to come from within, and we consider ourselves to be ordinary members of the public. We see crowdmapping as a way to decentralise activism on the issue away from experts and policymakers, who often view society as a passive beneficiary, and restore an active role for society in addressing the problem on its own behalf. For the first time in Egypt, HarassMap's crowdmap offered a free and easy tool for providing a direct means to voice sexual harassment experiences safely and anonymously. Speaking out, HarassMap's co-founders had learned during their work on the issue prior to HarassMap, was very often the first step to activism.

Crowdmapping has, however, been only one element in our approach since the beginning. More than 'just a map', HarassMap simultaneously launched a community mobilisation program to train and coordinate anti-harassment activism in neighbourhoods, interactive social media outreach and media relations, all designed to build off of each other, and the crowdmap to convince people to stand against sexual harassment and to deter harassers. The system also bridged a gap, sending victims an auto-response about existing but little-known services like legal aid and psychological counselling. Finally, the reports and map provided evidence for volunteers to mobilise bystanders to create neighbourhood 'safe areas' in which sexual harassment would not be tolerated.

Although victims of sexual harassment submit the most reports, we believe that victims don't cause sexual harassment, so bystanders are our primary big-picture target. In the early years of planning HarassMap, the co-founders had already experienced the unproductive, defensive reactions of harassers when confronted directly. In contrast, bystanders in Egypt are powerful. Shopkeepers, doormen, police, other women, people parking cars, drinking tea and socialising are always in the street and watching over their neighbourhoods. In the past, these were the people who would be the first to assist people in need of help, and even chase down harassers and shave their heads as a mark of shame. At this point, however, bystanders often ignored harassers, blamed the harassed or joined in the harassment. HarassMap volunteers sought to open conversations with these bystanders through both our online and offline activities, hoping to remind them of the traditional view of harassing behaviour as morally unacceptable and to revitalise positive intervention in cases of sexual harassment.

Using the map and reports to convince people to take the issue seriously and to challenge stereotypes that served as excuses, volunteers from all Egypt's governorates worked within their neighbourhoods to attract agents of change who are willing to shift their behaviour, in the hope of reaching a 'tipping point' and affect a wider crowd. HarassMap trained, coordinated and supported the volunteers, echoing their messages and experiences through social media, encouraging conversations, such as #EndSH and further encouraging the public to start sharing their sexual harassment experiences.

Putting Sexual Harassment on the Map

Functionally, as we launched the crowdmapping tool, a victim or witness of sexual harassment with access to the internet was able to go to the HarassMap website and fill in a form with details of what happened and where an incident occurred, without having to enter any personal information. The reporter could pinpoint the location of the incident through a text-based address search that populated the map, or by manually moving the map pin to the correct position. The same reporting functionality was possible in a slightly more limited capacity through text message, e-mails and Twitter, which are linked to the map, albeit less smoothly and less reliably and without the location population feature. Reports submitted via e-mails and Twitter were added to the map manually by the HarassMap team.

Reports were screened to filter out 'spam' and those meeting our criteria—about sexual harassment and naming a specific location—appeared as a red dot on our map. Instantly visually understandable, the map helped to demonstrate the prevalence of the problem, not only visualising the number of reported incidents but also their spread across the country. Interactive features allow users to zoom in and out on the map as a whole or specific location and to click on individual dots to view details of reports (see Figure 7.1).

Figure 7.1: Image of HarassMap's new mapping platform launched in 2018. The map zooms in and out, showing more specific locations of incidents. Clicking on a dot displays the narrative of the individual report. *Source: HarassMap website.*

Sharing their stories through the reporting system, sometimes for the first time, victims documented their own experiences and showed others that they were not alone. They demonstrated in their voices that sexual harassment is widespread and traumatic. Perhaps, they did not or could not respond as they would have liked in the moment of the incident, but many have told us that reporting is a way to at least record that it happened, even if it was days, weeks or years later.

The crowdsourced data collected by HarassMap created an important evidence base of sexual violence in Egypt, different in content than data gathered face-to-face or through traditional research methods where people were often more hesitant to talk about the issue. These powerful stories—with direct, detailed and personal content—drew the attention of the media and shocked people who heard them. Reports came in from locations and demographics that had never been surveyed, providing evidence against stereotypes, for example, that sexual harassment is an urban phenomenon, that it only happens to women, that the victims are dressed provocatively, that they enjoy being harassed, that it only happens at night in isolated locations, or that only grown, uneducated, unmarried men are harassers. Using the content of reports to break stereotypes became an important element of our work. Stereotypes deflected responsibility onto the harassed, and came up consistently as excuses for bystanders to remain passive and for harassers to keep harassing.

Thanks to our reports, we were seeing data directly contradicting most myths. Reports came from people of all ages and social backgrounds. Reporters talked about the clothes they wore, showing that even women wearing abayas and covering their hair and face are targeted by harassers. They described their harassers, and in some cases, they were not men but women or children, proving that men's sexual frustration is not the cause of sexual harassment (a common excuse made for harassing behaviour). Harassers were doctors, professors, police, school children, drivers of expensive cars, in big cities and small villages and at all times of day, often in crowded places with many witnesses.

In addition to creating this safe space to speak out and find services, HarassMap pushed for greater social awareness of the problem, with the end goal of encouraging behavioural change. We tweeted out facts, posted quotes, held in-person events encouraging sharing of stories and designed public campaigns based on evidence from reports. The data, still anonymous, was open for researchers, other activists and the media to analyse and use. Our volunteers used it as well when they spoke to their neighbours, using reports to prove that actions are needed to be taken against harassment.

Before launching the platform, the founders had considered additional uses for the reported data but quickly decided against them. The first was to use the map to advocate, with police, for greater enforcement of sexual harassment laws in areas that received many reports. This would have resulted in reports having a direct effect on the ground, but the politicised nature of the issue was a barrier too big to overcome. We also considered targeting the so-called 'hotspots' for our community mobilisation activities. We abandoned this idea immediately when so many volunteers approached us and suggested that we could form neighbourhood teams instead, which would avoid any 'outsider' effect.

With the onset of the revolution in January 2011 and a profound problem of mass sexual violence in the Tahrir Square protests, volunteer efforts spiked. This was true not only in the case of HarassMap, but in the rising number of other volunteer-based sexual harassment initiatives that began to emerge at this time. At launch, more than 300 individuals sought to report and volunteer with HarassMap. This number grew to about 800 by 2012 and 1,200 by 2013, roughly speaking. During this time, HarassMap's crowdmap was often mentioned as one of the ways the extent of everyday nature of sexual harassment was effectively visualised and communicated, helping people sort fact from fiction, understand the broader non-politicised problem and turn their frustration into positive action.

The research component of HarassMap's work also grew to become an integral part of the organisation's work. Data derived from the crowdmap, field data, the experience of field staff, social media data and finally, data gathered for specific research projects implemented by the

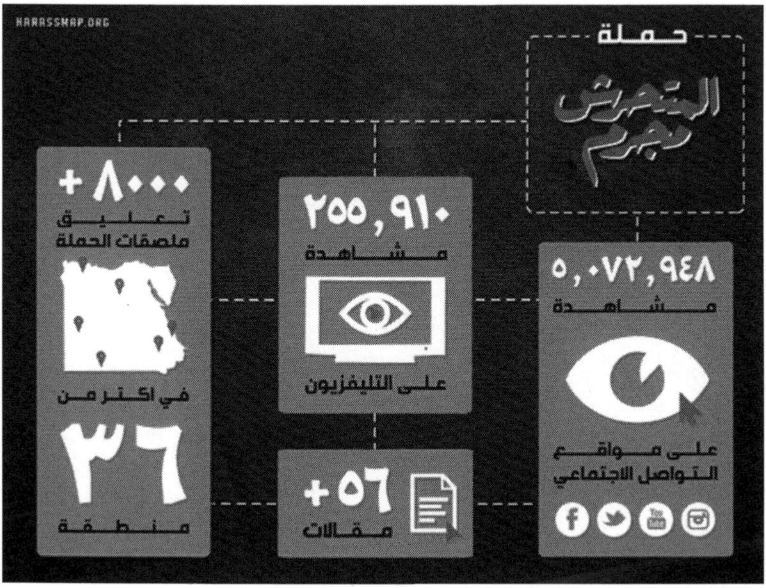

Figure 7.2: HarassMap infographic produced as part of the Harasser=Criminal campaign. Design by Riham Ali.

research team was analysed and crafted into campaigns and easy to understand visualisations (see Figure 7.2). It was also used internally, guiding HarassMap's strategic decisions, messaging and approach. For instance, in 2015, HarassMap investigated trends regarding sexual harassment at workplace, a project that coincided with the expansion of our Safe Corporates program. In 2017, a hashtag #FirstTimeIwasHarassed flooded the internet calling for stories from Egypt on sexual harassment against children. With the help of volunteers who collected the testimonies, HarassMap analysed trends found in this hashtag, helping to understand the dynamics of sexual harassment and abuse against children in Egypt, from the first dataset available to the public.

Strategies for Bystander Intervention

In neighbourhoods, 'Community Captains'—trained on the key facts HarassMap learned from the reports—led local volunteer teams on regular 'outreach days' targeting an area in their neighbourhood in which they would start conversations with the public on working together to create anti-harassment 'safe areas' where bystanders would intervene when witnessing sexual harassment. Occasional open mic days or theatrical productions to encourage community dialogue were also arranged by the 'captains' (see Figure 7.3).

Figure 7.3: HarassMap volunteers mobilising bystanders in their neighbourhoods to be watchful against harassment and help victims. Photos by HarassMap.

We constantly experimented with messaging and approach. Most questions raised by people reflected familiar stereotypes that were easily answered with report-data. HarassMap addressed the most common ones through public campaigns spread through social media and in the streets. The highly politicised nature of the issue and the rapidly changing political environment in Egypt—a revolution and four different governments in three-and-a-half years)—made it a constant challenge.

Figure 7.4: HarassMap posters (unbranded) from the Mesh Sakta campaign. Photo by HarassMap.

HarassMap's first message asked bystanders to be vigilant and intervene when they see sexual harassment. Later, we targeted popular stereotypes by asking 'if harassment is because of [a particular stereotype], then why does [counter evidence] exist'. Examples included 'if harassment is because of how women dress, then why do women who wear *niqab* get harassed?' and 'if harassment is because of low education, then why does a university professor harass?'

We compiled evidence from reports backing up each claim. Another campaign responded to feedback we received from bystanders who were unsure if people being harassed want their help. *Mesh Sakta*, or *'I will not be silent'*, encouraged women to ask for help, report and support each other when witnessing sexual harassment (see Figure 7.4). Our campaign 'Harasser=Criminal' shifted the stigma from the harassed to the act of harassment. The campaigns were disseminated online and in print, and used by volunteers in the streets, universities and workplaces; one of them also on TV and radio.

Although early volunteers reported that about eight in ten people they approached in their neighbourhoods were convinced and agreed to take action against sexual harassment, this rate was far from stable. Along with the co-opting of the issue by various political forces in order to accuse opponents of sponsoring sexual harassment, the motivations of volunteers and civil society organisations soon became suspect among the general public. Many people started to question the validity of anonymous reports and became hesitant to discuss or admit sexual harassment as a problem.

Impact measurement was also difficult for the community mobilisation volunteers. According to our plan, volunteers were to speak to bystanders and create zero-tolerance safe areas, returning several times to the same place to measure any perceptual and/or behavioural change and understand the impact. In practice, loaded with excitement, volunteers often moved from one bystander to the other, not keeping track of the people they visited. They wanted to tackle new and different places, making it impossible to measure the change in a specific geographic area.

Nonetheless, the teams brought back from the field many stories of engagement indicating significant work to change perceptions of people in the streets. Anecdotes also echoed the reports on our map and showed that a combination of facts and face-to-face dialogue on sexual harassment was triggering discussions and debates on the issue in the neighbourhoods. Some bystanders eventually acknowledged that sexual harassment is a problem and pledged to intervene when they see it.

As HarassMap grew, we became better at implementing and monitoring outreach activities. Over time, they also developed into the more institutionally focused Safe Areas program. The idea of Safe Areas was suggested to community mobilisation volunteers in December 2010 by a shop owner who wanted a way to advertise that his shop stood against sexual harassment. In response, we developed visibility materials for Safe Areas partners to display, and soon developed an anti-harassment policy and pledge, training for employees and a system for monitoring implementation. The idea evolved into a program, which then evolved into a unit that has worked with a large variety of institutions, from individual taxi drivers to multinational corporations such as Uber.

The Safe Areas unit—today consisting of Safe Corporates dealing with larger companies, Safe Areas dealing with community-level businesses and Safe Schools and Universities—functions with the same goal of creating and spreading spaces with zero tolerance to sexual harassment, but is targeting institutions instead of individuals in the open street. We adjust the anti-sexual harassment policies to suit the institution's size and mandate, train personnel with tailored content and follow up on the commitment of these partners. The biggest success of Safe Areas is the partnership with Cairo University, which adopted and implemented an anti-sexual harassment policy in 2014, and then spearheaded a nationwide anti-sexual harassment program between 2016 and 2018 that involved twelve public universities.

Reflections on Some Challenges of Crowdmapping

Crowdmapping has not been without its challenges. From the start, not having previous experience of working with technology or online tools, the co-founders faced numerous hurdles in setting up and linking Ushahidi, Frontline SMS and Wordpress (where the HarassMap website lived). They had to rely heavily on local and international volunteer technology partners. In October 2010, when the HarassMap crowdmapping tool and website went live for the first time for a pre-launch test, the unexpected volume of users accessing its content and submitting reports caused the website to almost immediately crash. Volunteers, some of them based on the other side of the world were called in to get it up and running again.

Among other pre-launch challenges was finding a way around the lack of specific hardware needed to set up Frontline SMS, which allowed text message reports to link to the Ushahidi crowdmap. The SMS phone number was long and difficult to remember, and we chose to work with a telecom that donated a short code for SMS reports. Language compatibility of the platform also needed a work-around to facilitate its English and Arabic interfaces. The public's unfamiliarity with the maps and formal addresses, as against rich descriptions of locations that are more common to the public, also proved challenging as reporters often struggled with pinpointing the correct location of an incident. In this sense, the map's feature itself, while proving to be valuable to visualise the problem in terms of numbers and geographical spread, also proved to be a practical challenge in terms of reporting and, as we later discovered, in the systematic analysis of the report data.

Pre-launch, the cofounders worried about false information and not having the capacity to implement a verification system while preserving the anonymity of reports. This was one issue that resolved itself. By reviewing each report before it was allowed to appear on the map, they quickly discovered that 'false' reports were few and obvious, either irrelevant or nonsensical. There was also no consequences to the reports: no legal action or follow-up to motivate people to send false information. Today, we have put a disclaimer on the site, removed information that compromises anonymity, and only allowed reports to appear publicly that met set criteria. We have also learned to proactively inform users of the specifics of the crowdsourced data and to what extent HarassMap does or does not have control over the content or nature of the reports.

Later, when HarassMap started a research unit to systematically examine the data we received, analysis of the crowdsourced reports became another hurdle. With a relatively open reporting form, the way different people reported was inconsistent and challenging to analyse for research purposes. Some sent just one word such as 'harassed'. Others sent pages of incidents collected into one report with details about the situations, contexts, their reactions, feelings at the time and the impact on them in the future, etc. In some instances, there were also discrepancies between the incident location as populated by the map feature and the description of the place of the incident in the narrative of the report.

Another major challenge has been encouraging people to submit reports. More than eight years after HarassMap's founding, roughly 1,500 reports have been submitted to the online platform. For a country of more than 90 million people where sexual harassment is a widespread problem, this is relatively low. We think there are many possible and intersecting reasons for this. One reason might be that we have chosen to de-emphasise the reporting system. To draw more attention to our offline work with community mobilisation and Safe Areas, we decided at one point to remove the reporting form and the map of the homepage and place it elsewhere on the HarassMap website. In public communications and campaigns, an emphasis was put on bystander intervention strategies and volunteering, not reporting. Additionally, access to online platforms such as ours is generally much lower than access to other forms of communication, such as television and radio. In Egypt, the television penetration rate as of 2010 was 94 per cent (Abdulla 2013), whereas internet penetration rate as of 2013 was roughly 30 per cent (MCIT 2015). Since people generally preferred to send reports via the internet rather than by SMS, access to the Internet has been critical.

More recently, the increase in smartphones, mobile apps and social media have contributed to a change in the landscape of reporting and talking about sexual harassment in Egypt. Despite issues with access, and due to the decrease in shame associated with sexual harassment, for example, Facebook has become an important space for many individuals to not only discuss their experiences of sexual violence without anonymity but also to voice their perspectives on the issue (Peuchaud 2014; Skalli 2014). Despite Facebook and HarassMap's crowdmapping tool both being online platforms, there has been a clear preference among the public to use social media rather than crowdmapping to talk about sexual harassment. Some of this may be attributable to Facebook's popularity and the public's lack of knowledge of HarassMap's crowdmap, especially given our de-emphasis on it, but may also be because of the way a web-based survey tool compares to a social platform also accessible on mobile. Especially, early on, users were required to respond to a series of questions before submitting a report, not unlike a survey. To what degree this deterred reporting is unclear, but has been a source of an ongoing conversation within HarassMap.

A key issue has also been managing people's expectations regarding reporting and communicating clearly what the impact of sending a report will be. Internally HarassMap dubbed this the 'why report' question. After progress was made on breaking some of the taboos around sexual harassment, the initial value of the reports for breaking the silence on sexual harassment lessened. The persistence and everyday occurrence of sexual harassment, despite some mobilisation against it, also demotivated reporting and has caused a sort of reporting-fatigue. Not seeing the immediate impact, many potential reporters have expressed that they feel 'there is no point' in reporting. Having already de-prioritised reporting and mapping by this point, we have struggled to adapt to the need to formulate a new, clear 'why report' message, causing some people to expect some direct intervention or action following a report and being disappointed or discouraged when that has not happened.

Other reasons might have to do with the technology itself. With the fast development of online tools and platforms, it is possible that HarassMap's anonymous system, the way it was initially built in 2010, lost value and attractiveness in an environment that only a few years after its launch became more open to discussions of sexual harassment experiences and more desiring of feedback, interaction and practical support. HarassMap's use of social media and crowdmapping has in this sense reflected the tensions that exist in the use of technology for and by social causes. The crowdmapping platform has been challenging to install, set-up, sync with SMS and website, and maintain over time, often requiring specialists to troubleshoot problems. With few local Ushahidi developers and no real internal technological knowledge, maintaining and updating the tool has always been difficult. The result was that there were periods when elements of reporting simply did not function and that very few updates were performed on the tool since its launch in 2010 up until 2017.

Our experience is that generating a higher volume of crowdmapped reports requires consistent and broad-based advertising of the platform with a clear reason why people should report and its impact on the larger problem. Without strategic priority given to such an effort for many years, the number of reports has remained relatively low.

Replication: New Global Crowdmapping Platform

Since launching, we have received requests from hundreds of activists and organisations in other countries to assist them with replicating our model. Because HarassMap's co-founders received so much help in setting up and growing over the years, it has always been important for us to support others requesting assistance. Although it was officially outside of our mission until 2016, the team has provided informal coaching sessions to groups and individuals to share knowledge and lessons learned. From 2010 to 2016, activists and organisations in over forty countries, including Jordan, Libya, Turkey, South Africa, US, Canada, Iran, Malaysia, Indonesia, Japan, Cambodia, Morocco, Saudi Arabia, Afghanistan, Kenya, Sudan, UK, India, Nigeria and a cross-national group from South America received advice, and some succeeded in setting up local versions of HarassMap.

Over the years we have worked to improve the assistance we give to others. A needs assessment we conducted in 2016 showed an almost universal need to do more in-depth work with the groups we have coached; and that, like with HarassMap itself, setting up and maintaining a crowdmap is often the main challenge. As part of our renewed focus on reporting and as a response to support the needs of other groups, we decided to create new, custom-made crowdmapping platform more tailored to our needs and context, and make shareability the main feature. The new platform is based on a domain alias system that is centrally maintained by HarassMaps, and in this way eliminates the need for each group to rely on in-house developers or IT resources. Groups locally customise and manage their versions or domain aliases, and their individual site appears to the public as independent reporting and mapping website. A comprehensive best practices and set-up guide, technical manual and videos walk groups mostly independently through the set-up.

At its core, the new platform works the same way as the original version—providing a space for witnesses and victims to anonymously report and map incidents. However, it also offers more interactive data visualisation, an option for users to interact with each other and with reports by creating user accounts, and a space for users to share, comment and discuss. It gives more focus on encouraging bystander interventions, allowing people to report 'positive' interventions on the crowdmap, in addition to sexual harassment incidents. Plans to map Safe Areas where anti-sexual harassment policies exist are also being made.

Since the launch of the new crowdmapping platform in late 2017, it has been adopted by initiatives in Egypt, Turkey, South Africa and Mexico, who use it to map and encourage action on sexual and gender-based violence, hate crimes and discrimination.

Concluding Thoughts

The silence around sexual harassment is slowly being broken. Sexual harassment and violence are being discussed in media, among friends and at workplaces and educational institutions. The issue continues to be part of public discourse and has not disappeared from the wider consciousness as between late 2008 and 2010. Many organisations and initiatives have emerged side by side with HarassMap since 2010 to fight sexual harassment in different and innovative ways. Crowdmapping, together with strong and innovative on-the-ground mobilisation, has been and continues to be at the core of HarassMap's work. The visibility of the crowdmapping component has varied over the years because of technical difficulties, strategic decisions to balance our online and offline work and the challenges of making crowdmapping a useful and impactful tool for change. However, the crowdmapped data has also helped to put sexual harassment on the map, for the first time in Egypt provided a space to talk about the issue and pushed it onto political agendas and into public discussion. It has played a key role in allowing HarassMap to create information material, run training and implement anti-sexual harassment policies to challenge stereotypes and transform attitudes and behaviour.

The need for safe reporting of sexual violence globally is as urgent as ever. The Me Too movement was, perhaps, an important reminder, and proof, that sexual violence is widespread and toxic, and that the silence around it needs to be broken over and over again. Through sharing our experiences and lessons learned, and making our crowdmapping platform open globally for others to use and develop, we want to contribute to this movement, not least by doing our part to make crowdmapping for social change more accessible, affordable and understandable.

Note

1. Ushahidi is a non-profit technology company with staff in nine countries whose mission is to help marginalised people raise their voice and those who serve them to listen and respond better. https://www.ushahidi.com/

References

Abdelhadi, Magdi. 'Cairo Street Crowds Target Women'. BBC, 1 November 2006. Accessed 9 January 2020 http://news.bbc.co.uk/2/hi/middle_east/6106500.stm

Abdelmonem, Angie. 'Reconceptualising Sexual Harassment in Egypt: A Longitudinal Analysis of El-Taharrush El-Ginsy in Arabic Online Forums and Anti-Sexual Harassment Activism'. *KOHL: A Journal for Body and Gender Research* 1, no. 1 (2015): 23–41. Accessed 9 January 2020 https://www.csbronline.org/?p=697

Abdulla, Rasha. *Mapping Digital Media: Egypt—A Report by the Open Society Foundation*. Open Society Foundation, 1 August 2013. Accessed 9 January 2020. https://www.opensocietyfoundations.org/sites/default/files/mapping-digital-media-egypt-20130823.pdf

El Mahdi, Rabab. 'Does Political Islam Impede Gender-Based Mobilisation? The Case of Egypt.' *Totalitarian Movements and Political Religions* 11, no. 3–4 (2010): 379–396.

FIDH, Nazra for Feminist Studies, New Women Foundation and the Uprising of Women in the Arab World. *Egypt: Keeping Women Out—Sexual Violence Against Women in the Public Sphere.* Joint Report, 2014. Accessed 29 January 2015 https://www.fidh.org/IMG/pdf/egypt_women_final_english.pdf

Goodchild, Michael F. and J. Alan Glennon. 'Crowdsourcing geographic information for disaster response: a research frontier'. *International Journal of Digital Earth* 3, no. 3 (2010): 231–241.

Hassan, Rasha, Nehad Aboul Qomsan and Aliyaa Shoukry. *Clouds in Egypt's Sky: Sexual Harassment from Verbal Harassment to Rape—A Sociological Study.* ECWR Report, 2008. Accessed 19 January 2015 https://egypt.unfpa.org/en/publications/clouds-egypts-sky-en

Hester, Vaughn, Aaron Shaw and Lukas Biewald. 'Scalable Crisis Relief: Crowdsourced SMS Translation and Categorisation with Mission 4636 (15)'. ACM Dev 2010—First ACM Symposium on Computing for Development, 17–18 December 2010.

Hussein, Abdel-Rahman. 'Stand Up for Your Rights, Says Victorious Noha Roushdy'. *Daily News Egypt*, 24 October 2008. Accessed 9 January 2020 https://dailynewsegypt.com/2008/10/24/stand-up-for-your-rights-says-victorious-noha-roushdy/

Ilahi, Nadia. 'You Got to Fight for Your Rights: Street Harassment and Its Relationship to Gendered Violence, Civil Society, and Gendered Negotiations'. MA Thesis, Department of Anthropology, Sociology, Psychology and Egyptology, American University in Cairo, 2008. Accessed 19 January 2015 http://dar.aucegypt.edu/bitstream/handle/10526/3259/Ilahi_Thesis_AUC.pdf?sequence=1

Kahl, Anne, Christy McConnell and William Tsuma. 'Crowdsourcing as a Tool in Conflict Prevention'. *Conflict Trends* 1 (2012): 27–34.

MCIT. *Measuring the Digital Society in Egypt: Internet at a Glance.* Arab Republic of Egypt, Ministry of Communications and Information Technology, 2015. Accessed 9 January 2020 http://www.mcit.gov.eg/Upcont/Documents/Publications_1272015000_Measuring_the_Digital_Society_in_Egypt_12_.pdf

Peuchaud, Sheila. 'Social Media Activism and Egyptians' Use of Social Media to Combat Sexual Violence: An HiAP Case Study'. *Health Promotion International* 29, no. 1 (2014): i113–i120.

Rizzo, Helen, Anne M. Price and Kathrine Meyer. 'Anti-Sexual Harassment Campaign in Egypt'. *Mobilization* 17, no. 4 (2012): 457–475.

Skalli, Loubna Hanna. 'Young Women and Social Media Against Sexual Harassment in North Africa'. *The Journal of North African Studies* 19, no. 2 (2014): 244–258.

8

FEMINIST SOLIDARITY THROUGH MAPPING (FEMMAP)

Interview with Juliana Guarany da Cunha Santos, by Siddharth Peter de Souza

FemMap is a platform created to document and connect feminist projects with the intention of providing inputs from similar projects that could help one another. The idea was to develop a community of practitioners that would interact, ask and answer questions regarding their projects and help one another on common issues.

Could you tell us a little bit about how FemMap came to be? What motivated you to start the platform?
FemMap emerged as a result of research on a series of digital projects around feminist activism. I remember looking at questions of street harassment and found projects such as HarassMap in Egypt, Chega de Fiu Fiu in Brazil, and iHollaback in the US. Many of them documented and reported cases using very similar technologies and approaches. What surprised me was that these projects all seemed to start from scratch. They were projects that, on the face of it, did not connect with each other, but rather existed as standalone projects without any collaborations. Through my research, I found that it would be very useful to connect these different projects to find ways for them to talk to each other, to talk about work, to even, maybe, help each other out. There are so many ideas out there that need to be spread: activists in India or Brazil can learn from activists in Egypt, and through this technology of connecting these different platforms, FemMaps aimed to build solidarity and learning between different projects and, through sharing knowledge, different projects would learn from each other and their challenges and mistakes.

Was there something in your own lifeworld in Brazil that sparked an interest in working on these issues? How did you become interested in these issues?
In 2010, after I moved out of Brazil for the first time at the age of thirty, and came to Germany, I realised that I could walk down the street without anybody looking or saying anything to me. I found this very hard to imagine. That was how complicated things are in Brazil. It was really bothering me that I hadn't questioned these issues enough, and so when I went back to Brazil, I realised I needed to do something. Two days after my return, with my guard down, I was walking down the street and a guy said some awful things to me. They were really disgusting and I thought, 'Why do I have to hear this guy talking to me like that—and he thinks this is normal? Why do all women need to put up with this? What makes men think that they can do this?'

When I discussed this issue nobody initially listened, and many felt I was exaggerating. However, as we started talking among friends, we realised we all go through very similar experiences. Some thought it was normal to face this kind of harassment, but others started questioning it. Talking about our experiences and raising awareness was one thing we could do. What was amazing, though, was that around 2012, suddenly everyone was talking about their experiences, it was as if everybody in Brazil was a feminist. Since 2012, there has been a revolution in Brazil, of women just starting to speak up and talk about their experiences. While initially events like slut walks did not get much support, in 2012 or 2013 things really took off. The issue of street harassment and how men behave in public spaces started to raise eyebrows. Also, their attitudes towards women in bars and clubs were being called out. In general, men were being warned that they are not entitled to treat women as a 'piece of meat' anymore.

Did you see FemMap as something that began in Brazil or something global? Was it meant to look at particular kind of projects or was it more inclusive and open ended? Why did you use a map?
For me, I saw many things taking place and many incidents gaining importance. Brazil was definitely part of it. I was surprised by how things took off. While in the Western world—Canada, US, Germany, UK and

Australia—there were events such as slut walks, things suddenly took off in the developing world also, whether this was in Brazil or Egypt or India. There were many feminist movements coming to life, young girls were coming out as feminist, and I found all this very interesting. There were discussions about being a radical feminist or being moderate or whatever, but these were not as important for me. What was crucial was how mainstreamed issues related to women's rights were becoming and how it was percolating to everyday life.

To your question on who FemMaps were for, I felt it could be a space for everybody. FemMap was aimed to be global in its essence: projects from different countries don't usually compete with each other for attention or funding, so they can help with no consequences. Anyone could be on it, and place their own projects on it and get connected. It was meant to be like a hub where different projects across a wide spectrum of ideologies could come together to connect, share and grow. Using a map was also important to build a community because we felt that through this approach it would be more dynamic than just a page. Through adding projects, participants would also think about how to categorise their projects and look for similar projects like theirs, either in their own countries or even across the world. Solidarity would be achieved by transferring knowledge. For example, when a street harassment app was launched in Brazil, the American app called them and said 'you could have asked me for the code, I would have given it to you.' So if there was this sentiment among feminists, they should work together. But this was impossible to achieve with such a small budget.

We also had difficult experiences in trying to build the database. In one instance, we had a project with a group of radical feminists who didn't like the way we had written about their work; and rather than discussing how to make it better, it became aggressive, with them even trolling our team. It sort of was a telling incident because it was quite antithetical to the whole solidarity project that we were trying to develop.

Coming back to your use of a map as a device for this project, why did you think this was the appropriate device for such a project?

There's a phrase I used to use with respect to the project, and it was about balance. When you go too deep, you don't go too far. And when you go very far, you don't go too deep. So what I chose was a world-wide angle, because I realised I didn't have the resources to go too deep. So my idea was to document. I just wanted to show how many projects there were, and just show how huge this community is and how similar the problems are everywhere. Through this, it was meant to build solidarity. I aimed to keep it free and just allow different groups to connect.

For populating the map, I asked my developer to create a form for people to write about their projects. I told him I wanted the simplest thing possible: just name and date pointers on a map. However, he ended up creating such a massive form, with over twenty questions for every project to answer, plus he put a password for people to create accounts. It raised barriers towards using the map from our users.

What was your funding situation like? What did you use the funding for?

All my funding for the project came from the Alexander von Humboldt Foundation. As part of my German Chancellor Fellowship, my host university was given money for my project, which they allowed me to use to build the website and hire two assistants. My team helped to insert projects on the map, to write blog entries, as well as to post on Facebook. As I was pregnant at the time, this was a great help to get the platform up and running.

Can you tell us a bit about the design of the platform? How did you make it engaging?

Did you think it was engaging? I have always had mixed emotions with the map. Part of me is concerned that people wouldn't use it. When we built it, we wanted it to be a stylish version of Google maps. So, if you have visited the platform you would see the different continents and the numbers of projects on these different continents, and people could intuitively get a sense of the kind of work that is going on. However, we also found it quite difficult to populate the map in practical terms; sometimes this was because of small things like the details of filling out the different projects with particular addresses, then the question was about data, we didn't want to put people's personal information and addresses online. We just wanted information regarding their projects and an approximate of where they were located. It was a Google-based map, so it needed an address for every project. Sometimes we would have the same location for several projects and that became a problem. But when you insert a project, it would show up on the map. One could click on it to find out more about it, and also to see other similar ideas related to it.

We also had a big challenge, however, in getting other people to document stories. We tried to make it as simple as possible, but we ended up having to document many of the projects ourselves.

This was one of the constant discussions I had with my developer. I asked him to reduce the barriers as much as possible so that many people would use it. But we found out that because we had elements such as asking people for their names and passwords before they could enter projects, they were not willing to work on the site.

Did you have to moderate any stories? Did you have a process in place when others not part of your team added stories?

We did not really have a problem of moderation because we were never able to get as many people on board to add stories. However, when we did, we would check everything, not just fact-checking but also proofreading. Even when we reached out to organisations and asked them to check our entries, we often found that they felt like it was additional work for them, and hence perhaps we need to brainstorm more on why this platform could be advantageous for them.

How did you build the outreach for FemMap? Did you have an advocacy or PR strategy?

We did some work on PR by writing articles about it. We connected with other feminist outlets and were able to build a following of over 3,000 people on Facebook; it's not a big following, but it is substantial, and we found that there was interest, but we had to make it sustainable.

We also tried mainstream media but many of them didn't pick it up. We tried online and we tried newspapers, but it didn't work, and we found that disappointing. On reflection, we found that it may have been because it was a bit of a niche topic, and the fact that newspapers were inundated with many press releases made it more difficult for them to take this seriously.

In Brazil, another challenge was the language—the fact that it was in English. But we wanted to focus on the world map because this was one way for Brazilian activists also to access the world. But of course, the cost was the language. A project in English can only go so far. All non-English speaking countries would just not get into the project, including Brazil.

Finally, what is the idea of FemMap going forward?

We were brainstorming on these issues and decided that we should adopt a new approach to help more people connect and use the platform. One of our ideas was to set up something simple like a Facebook group and just connect many people as they are already on that platform; and then additionally, from that platform take stories to feed FemMaps. Because, if we can get the group going and start talking then the website can always develop. The key idea, however, is to start a conversation whether on a map or a group.

I still think mapping could work, but the problem is that a project like this needs a lot of marketing, and needs to be done properly. I don't have the resources to properly do it. Honestly, it should be a major institute's project, like the UN Women. The historical part is relevant for them, and the hub would make it much easier to fund projects. There's much we can do going forward, but maybe it needs a much bigger push.

We want people to know that they have a community and that they have support when they take a stand. After all, we want FemMap to create solidarity with people around the world.

PART IV

CIVIC ENGAGEMENTS

9

CORRUPTION AND CROWDSOURCING

Reflections on I Paid a Bribe

Sumit Arora, Sandhya Christabel D'Souza and Dheeman Ghosh

Introduction

I Paid a Bribe (IPAB) is an initiative started by the Janaagraha Centre for Citizenship and Democracy to uncover the market price of corruption in India through data provided by citizens. It is a platform for people to report the nature, number, pattern, types, location, frequency and values of actual corrupt acts such as bribery in government agencies affecting fruitful governance on the website ipaidabribe.com. The web portal then aggregates the data to create maps and charts of corrupt activities across Indian cities. Through visualising the data, the project aims to build awareness and create a sense of accountability, regarding the cost of corruption. The data so collected reflects the corruption scenario of bribes occurring in Indian cities. The data will be used for improving governance systems and procedures, tightening law enforcement and regulation, thereby reducing the scope for corruption in obtaining services from the government.

IPAB is a form of data journalism, with a view to identify report and define the scope of corruption in relation to public services in the country. Beyond conventional storytelling, IPAB became a platform for victims of retail corruption to speak about the experiences they faced at the hands of bureaucratic and political forces. It is a tool for participatory governance, as people have an opportunity to voice out against illegitimate transactions at the organisational level of public service delivery.

IPAB has emerged and evolved over time. It commenced with a discussion between the co-founders of Janaagraha, Swati and Ramesh Ramanathan, and a member of the Janaagraha's advisory board, Sridar Iyengar, on the pernicious effect of corruption, and how it is destroying city life and disempowering citizens. Corruption poses a tremendous challenge for a developing country like India. According to the

Global Corruption Barometer for the Asia Pacific Region released by Transparency International (TI) on 7 March 2017 in Berlin, India has the highest bribery rate among the sixteen Asian countries surveyed. Nearly seven in ten people who accessed public services in India had paid a bribe. India had the highest bribery rates of all the countries surveyed for access to public schools (58 per cent) and healthcare (59 per cent), suggesting serious corruption risks when people try to access these basic services. The Corruption Perception Index of Transparency International for 2017 awarded India a score of 40, rendering it the 81st most corrupt country in the world.

Although corruption has become an increasingly important issue over the past few decades, there is no real system to address it. Discussing corruption and bribery is still a taboo since even the most honest of people are forced to resort to dishonest means in extreme situations.

Janaagraha Centre for Citizenship and Democracy is a not-for-profit organisation established in 2001. The organisation works with citizens to catalyse active participation in city neighbourhoods, and with state governments to institute reforms in city governance. Civic learning, civic participation and advocacy and reforms are Janaagraha's three major strands of work towards accomplishing its mission. IPAB is one of Janaagraha's initiatives that aims to increase people's participation in democracy and governance. The initial idea of IPAB was to create a web platform that would act as a means of tracking the market price of corruption—a kind of *mandi* (Hindi word for business or market) for price prediction mechanism. People in Delhi, for example, have paid Rs 500–1,000 for police verification of passports. Those in Mumbai have paid anything between Rs 20 to as high as Rs 21 lakh as bribes to the police. IPAB uses a crowdsourcing model to collect bribe reports and to build a repository of corruption-related data across government departments.

The original idea was propelled more by tongue-in-cheek humour. A small experimental website was launched in order to test the idea. However, as the project progressed, there was a realisation that such an effort could be much more powerful. The website has moved beyond only giving the market price for corruption to undertaking a detailed analysis of process workflows, identifying corruption-prone processes and suggesting reforms to eliminate these. The idea gained acceptance and the team at IPAB worked on making the idea more user-friendly by adding a lot more features.

The website was relaunched on 15 August 2010, India's Independence Day. The new site was multi-faceted, providing a wide range of services to citizens, allowing them to report on the nature, number, pattern, types, locations and frequency of actual corrupt acts and values of bribes, which will add to a valuable knowledge bank that will contribute to the reduction in bribe payments.

The initiative of IPAB fits into the overall objective of Janaagraha, which works for improving the quality of citizenship, infrastructure and services in Indian cities. IPAB has aligned itself with Janaagraha's goal of making a measurable difference in the quality of citizenship in cities. It does this by adopting the strategy of empowering citizens using what we call a 'net-plus-roots' approach. We use an Internet-based platform for recording grassroots experiences of citizens. IPAB aims to heighten citizens' awareness of the nature and spread of bribe-related exchanges and to promote a purposive public debate that pressurises public officials to reduce and eventually eliminate corruption, helping citizens to recognise, avoid and tackle bribe paying situations. It identifies and analyses the workflows within corruption prone public services to make suggestions on systemic reform directed at entrenching simpler and more transparent processes, more consistent standards of law enforcement and better vigilance and regulation.

By gathering bribe reports from the citizens themselves, this platform enables people to be sensitive to the gravity of corruption problems in the country, and also allows them to contribute towards mitigating the problems affecting good governance. In the following sections, we look at some important issues the platform seeks to address: the means and challenges of gathering data, uses of social media, addressing questions of neutrality and bias on the platform, aspects of visualisation that are important to the platform and how we use the platform for dissemination and advocacy.

Means and Challenges of Gathering Data

Data selection and curation

Collection of data on corruption from first-hand experiences of citizens forms the basis of the functioning of the IPAB portal. Crowdsourcing reports is a unique method, as it highlights various loopholes in the system and also different situations where people have become victims of bribery. The reports will, perhaps for the first time, provide a snapshot of bribes occurring across Indian cities. IPAB will use the data to argue for improving governance systems and procedures, tightening law enforcement and regulation, thereby reducing the scope for corruption in obtaining services from the government. The portal gets about twenty-five to fifty reports every day in the sections 'I Paid a Bribe', 'I Am a Bribe Fighter' and 'I Met an Honest Official' (see Figure 9.1).

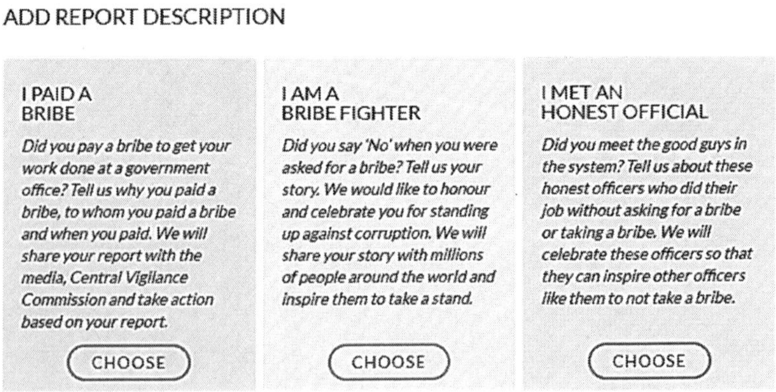

Figure 9.1: Types of reporting available online for a user to share bribe experiences.
Source: I Paid a Bribe website.

Under the 'I Paid a Bribe' section, reporters have an option to select areas of government functioning. These areas consist of almost all areas where governments provide services to citizens; therefore, citizens' interactions with their governments' agencies are crucial to the execution of governance.[1] Once an area is chosen, there is an option to select specific reasons that come under the ambit of the focus area. These filters or areas allow for easy categorisation and analysis of data. This form of collection of data makes it easier to tabulate statistics of overall country reports (see Figure 9.2).

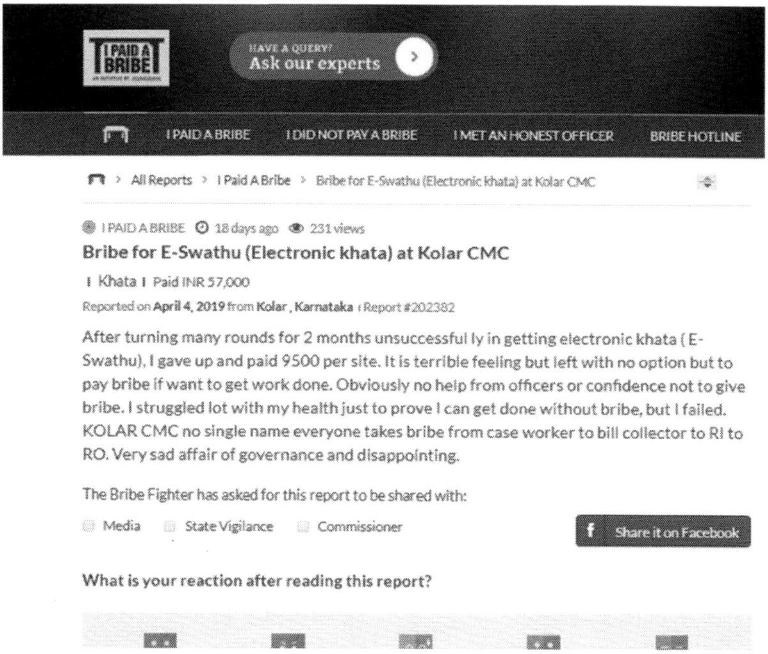

Figure 9.2: An example of a bribe paid report.
Source: I Paid a Bribe website.

Providing a space for people to speak about corruption is only one facet of IPAB. The larger aim is to use the data to make detailed recommendations to various government departments across cities all over India, on how governments can eliminate avenues of corruption. As the data repository grows, the team has started to analyse various trends of improving public service delivery to make it more transparent and accountable, begun to put suggestions in public domain and also send recommendations to concerned departments suggesting policy interventions that could help in cleaning up the system with respect to specific areas of governance such as the regional transport office (RTO) or the sub-registrar's office. IPAB focuses on collaborating with the government on systemic reforms which are upstream and critical in creating channels for improved governance to emerge. We are also willing to work hand in hand with governments, in order to design systems, write new regulations. For example, based on our findings with regard to the transport department of Bengaluru, and subsequent engagement with the then transport commissioner, Bhaskar Rao, we were able to help the department revamp its citizens' charters as well as redesign its website to make it more user-friendly. We continued our engagement with officers to reduce corruption in the department.

IPAB was invited by the chief secretary of Karnataka to make a presentation before officials of the departments of transport, stamps and registration and electricity supply. The presentation focused on corruption in these departments and recommendations for reducing such corruption.

Except for using data that we receive for further analysis, we do not take individual complaints and stories forward. On the basis of the analysis, we engage positively with any arm of the government with a view to improve services and reduce the possibility of corruption.

The map section of the site gives a bird's eye view of the corruption scenario in the country. Unlike text-heavy reports, the map provides an easy visual guide to the data, accessible to a wider range of people. Whenever a corruption report is lodged, as per demographic details entered, the information is recorded under that particular state.

Social media and other forms of information

Other than the earlier mentioned categories of collecting information, IPAB uses Facebook and Twitter as major vehicles of information dissemination to get out words about our initiative and the pressing problem of corruption. IPAB frequently posts on Facebook and Twitter about issues of corruption in the country and from across the world, with the aim of reducing the menace.

On social media, we share web links of corruption news as well as corruption reports that are posted on the IPAB portal. With interesting posts, we encourage people to speak out about bribe and ask them to post reports on ipaidabribe.com.

IPAB started the '*Mujse Hogi Shuruvaat*' (Change begins with me) campaign in collaboration with the Shankar Mahadevan Academy and released a music video[2] that shows various instances of corruption taking place in the society and how citizens can spark a change. This, too, was a means of spreading the word out on social media to inspire people to act. For instance, IPAB held a live session on Facebook with two experts on corruption—Malati Das, former IAS officer and chief secretary of planning and statistics and S.T. Ramesh, former DG and IG, Karnataka—who spoke on the impact of demonetisation on retail corruption and bribery as reported on IPAB. They spoke on their analyses of the IPAB reports by collating data from four months before and after the demonetisation. Their analyses point out that though the quantum of bribe amount collected decreased post demonetisation, instances of public servants seeking bribes shot up by 10 per cent.

Corruption in India also persists because of citizens' lack of education and awareness of government processes and services. The 'How to' section on the website provides a platform that seeks to increase awareness among citizens about the functions of different areas of the government, such as passport, railways, etc. in order to enable citizens to be informed and fight corruption. It provides answers on how to access various government services.

When one knows how a government office functions, what are the steps to get different procedures done, what is the fee payable, one cannot be fooled and can fight corruption. To this end, IPAB includes a 'How to' section, which is regularly updated with explanations about different procedures in government departments, such as how to register a house, how to get a driving license and many more. With this information, people can be confident and can raise their voice when misled.

In the 'I Didn't Pay a Bribe' section of the website, many people have posted their experiences of successfully resisting corruption.

Champion of change

Even when corruption is rampant, there are individuals combating it in their daily lives. They have successfully outsmarted, out-argued or outwitted the corrupt. Having overcome the fear factor, they have refused to be misled or confused, done their homework and been very firm and patient in their resolve. They have often achieved success keeping their sense of humour intact, overcoming the scepticism of those that surround them. Such stories, like those of Manik Taneja who had to pay bribe under dire circumstances and took up a fight against the officer who arm-twisted him[3] are highlighted on the website as a means of creating a positive narrative.

Addressing Neutrality and Bias

In reporting any bribe, complete autonomy is given to the reporter. He/she is allowed to choose options such as the government department, the concerned area/work for which bribe was asked, city, amount, date and a brief description of the incident. Also, the reporter has a choice to remain anonymous or to give his/her personal details. In this way, the portal protects the interests of a bribe reporter. This feature encourages him/her to be honest while reporting a bribe and also removes the fear factor.

The problem of bias persists in the platform, however. Access to such a portal is not uniform and widespread—the reports may reflect corruption situations of only certain parts of the country (say urban), or maybe only from a certain class of society. For instance, when you refer to our maps, the maximum amount of corruption appears to be reported in Karnataka. However, this could be for many reasons, including the fact that Bengaluru in Karnataka is an IT hub, and computer literacy is higher here. This likely facilitates greater online engagement among citizens but does not necessarily reflect the proportion of corruption in Karnataka versus in other states.

Keeping in mind these problems, the portal has the facility to report both bribes and honest officers. This in a way is to try and understand not only negative experiences with governance but also to document constructive experiences. It allows for a sense of citizen empowerment while ensuring that officers working in various areas of the government are not misrepresented.

The number of people with access to the Internet is growing by leaps and bounds in India. According to a report by Internet and Mobile Association of India (IAMAI) and Kantar IMRB, the number of Internet users stood at 481 million in December 2017 and was

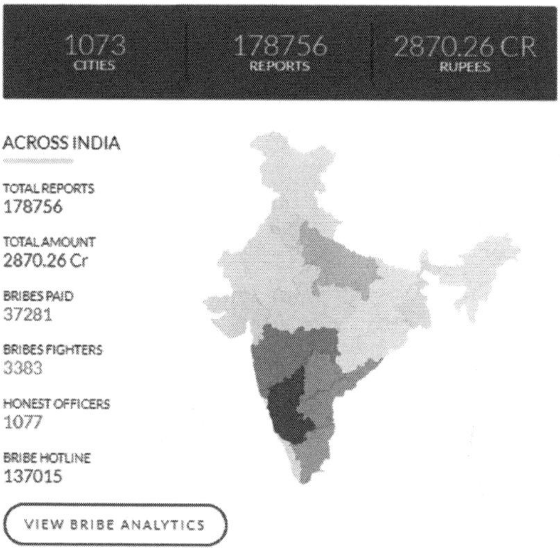

Figure 9.3: A screenshot of bribe reports as of 22 April 2019.
Source: I Paid a Bribe website.

predicted to touch 500 million by June 2018. An online platform to tackle corruption is a modern and efficient way to solve the problem of corruption. The main hurdle in this process is the lack of awareness among people about the existence of such a portal. For example, it can be seen that according to the statistics on the IPAB website, the maximum reports are reported in Karnataka. This, however, does not mean that the maximum number of bribes are given in Karnataka. The popularity of the website in the state is much higher than in other states, as the platform was launched in the state and gained maximum publicity there. In India, we are witnessing a phenomenon by which the Internet has become a rallying point for mass movements against corruption. IPAB has been an important part of this phenomenon because we provide a platform for citizens to report their stories and experiences regarding corruption (see Figure 9.3). However, given that we are present only online currently, we do realise our limitation to only reach people who have access to the Internet, who are still in a minority in India. However, this number is likely to grow rapidly in India; therefore, we hope our influence will spread even more. Efforts are being made to increase our outreach and to make people aware that they can report such situations in the IPAB web portal, such as '*Mujse Hogi Shuruvaat*' (Change begins with me) music video in collaboration with Shankar Mahadevan Academy, which motivates people to voice out against corruption.[4]

Relationship Between the Structural and Everyday

The IPAB program seeks to find out:

1. Whether bribe is collusive. 'Collusive corruption' is one in which there is a willing bribe giver who emerges as a 'formidable' challenge for institutions fighting corruption.
2. Whether citizens are being forced to pay bribes. In light of this, it is necessary to address the relationship between bribes reported in structural and everyday situations.

When crowdsourced reports are compared with real-time reports, such as the ones revealed by the government, especially when asked using the RTI tool, there is a huge disparity between the two datasets (see Figure 9.4). This reflects the presence of a divide, either due to technology or economy. For example, in everyday situation such as rail or road transport, everyone, irrespective of his or her financial background, is found in a similar situation. Therefore, in such an everyday situation, the numbers do not display a huge deviation. But when it comes to certain sectors, say the stamps and registration processes, it is only a certain class of people, generally the financially well-off, who opt for such services. So, although they might report instances of bribe online, the probability of them reporting the same during a ground research project is much less.

IPAB Crowdsourced Retail Bribery Index (CRBI) is a survey based on data collected between 2010 and 2013 from its reporting platform and compared with an on-the-ground survey by considering the same number of factors and parameters. It has been named as the Retail Bribe Index (RBI) and published in the form of facts and figures, which revealed some interesting results as depicted in Figure 9.4.[5] The survey data aims to give a better understanding to the question whether the trends emerging from the crowdsourced data available on IPAB are

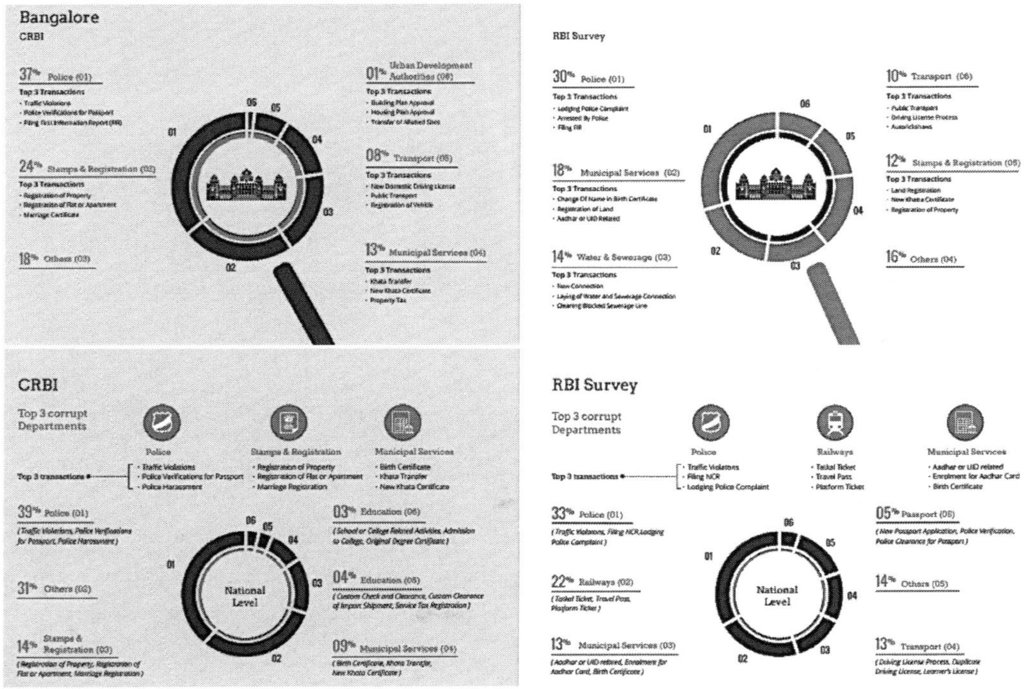

Figure 9.4: IPAB Crowdsourced Retail Bribery Index (CRBI) highlighting the top three bribe transactions across public departments (top left). Retail Bribery Index (RBI) survey highlighting the top three bribe transactions across public departments (top right). IPAB Crowdsourced Retail Bribery Index (CRBI) survey indicating the top three corrupt departments (bottom left). The top three corrupt public service departments according to Retail Bribery Index (RBI) survey (bottom right).

Source: I Paid a Bribe authors.

representative, and whether the website can act as a robust indicator of corruption rates over time. This is an important contribution to understanding the accuracy and role of crowdsourced data broadly, as well as expanding the reach of IPAB for policy advocacy work in the corruption space.

The following comparisons are between the percentage breakdown of bribes across departments as seen in the IPAB data, through CRBI, and as seen in the survey data conducted in Mumbai, Bengaluru and New Delhi through RBI. For each city surveyed for RBI, over 2,000 individuals per city were interviewed, giving a confidence level of 95 per cent and a confidence interval of +/− 2 per cent.

Although launching such a unique portal has its own challenges in terms of access, reach and authenticity of data, till date the IPAB website has recorded 1,46,766 bribe reports from nearly 1,071 cities in the country.

Visualisation: The Visual Aspects of Mapping

Tools and methods of visualisation

As part of the visualisation, IPAB uses primarily two components, namely the home page map visualisation of bribe distribution and a separate bribe analytics page. Maps are used to give a better perspective. It can give the viewer a sense of personalisation, making them easily grasp where their city/state stands. Nonetheless, this comes with the caveat that the state where more complaints are reported is not necessarily the most corrupt.

For the home page map visualisation of bribe distribution, IPAB involves a map view of India based on the state-specific demarcation of bribe distribution based on the attributes of total reports; total amounts; number of bribe payers, bribe fighters and honest officers; and bribe hotline (responses to 'how to' queries automated).

Moreover, one needs to note from the differential shades of grey depicting the number of reports. The darker the shade, the more the number of reports submitted. On our platform, Karnataka has the highest number of reports, which does not necessarily mean that it has the highest degree of retail corruption; but since the *awareness* of the reporting platform is the maximum here we have received most report inputs.

It is important to note that we provide our site visitors with visualisation of the map for understanding not only the state-wide view but also through a depiction of the national statistics on the top bar.

For the viewer, this creates a distinct idea of the significance and criticality of tackling 'petty' corruption and the gravity of the situation across the nation.

The noteworthy feature that IPAB has in terms of mapping is the bribe analytics page, which is linked to the 'View Bribe Analytics' clicker on the home page. The user can immediately visualise crowdsourced bribe data based on two features: bribes mapped in terms of cities and bribes mapped in terms of departments. Here, whenever a citizen posts a bribe report, he or she has to also enter the department, state and bribe amount details. This will help automatically update the bribe trends, such as the number of reports from each city and the amount of bribe collected. According to IPAB's analytics, the highest number of bribe instances and bribe amount is reported in Bengaluru. However, the analytics reflect the crowdsourced data. Bengaluru is featured on top as people in this city are more aware of IPAB. The department-wise data gives an understanding as to which department has maximum bribe grievances from citizens. Moreover, the bribe analytics page also helps the user to find further visuals containing city-specific information, for example, Bengaluru is shown in Figure 9.5.

Figure 9.5: Graphical illustration of the reporting trends of IPaidABribe from all crowdsourced reports across Bengaluru.

Source: I Paid a Bribe website.

One of the major drawbacks of the visualisation aspects of mapping bribe information has been that it does not show the density of bribes paid per area. This is a feature that has been seen in certain newer applications such as WhistleBlower, an app developed by the Government of Kerala, a state in southern India, which shows region-specific bribe information of different towns and cities across the state. Meanwhile, IPAB showcases bribe trends throughout the state and is not city-specific in bribe analytics. However, in the visualisation map, it shows the state-wise density.

A second issue is of data invisibility. The state-wise data is shown across India, but state information cannot be further analysed by clicking and selecting from the map itself. Another important limitation is in terms of exhaustive statistical representation, as in, graphical representation of all departments/cities and not just the major ones.

The Technologies of the Project

The key highlights of the technologies of the project are:

1. Quick and easy deployment

The software interface can be deployed in the signee country by easy login through single admin username and password, which will give access to all features and attributes that can be populated by the host country based on their data inputs even within twenty-four hours.

2. Easy update and maintenance

The 'software as a service' interface involves a guide document inbuilt on the backend, which provides effective information both on the key components of the site as well as processes in developing similar components for the signing organisation (such as our international partners) who want to build similar sites. These guide-features also enable our technical personnel such as the information technology personnel to troubleshoot problems and fix bugs in coding.

3. Bandwidth on demand

Depending on the requirement of site features by our international partners, IPAB can provide the necessary bandwidth on demand.

4. Localisation

It can be coded in any language used globally from the 'software as a service' backend-universal usage based on host countries/international partners' national language. This also supports alphabets not only in the English script but others as well, like Mandarin, Bengali, Arabic, etc.

IPAB has partnered with thirty countries to create replica IPAB sites, and hence it is part of an international Crowdsourcing Against Corruption Coalition. Interested organisations have contacted IPAB to start the platform in their respective countries. Janaagraha helps partner-organisations launch the site by sharing the user interface. The content can be changed into the partner country's native language. Janaagraha also helps partner countries to mentor their data and analytics and addresses their issues and concerns.[6]

Public Attention and Reception

Ipaidabribe.com aligns itself with Janaagraha's key thrust of increasing the number of citizens as change agents in the cities. Janaagraha believes that every citizen who reports a story on the website about having paid a bribe is angry enough to begin to resist it. Of course, it goes without saying that somebody who has resisted paying a bribe and reported the story is already very much on the path of being an agent of change.

Users can access bribe analytics and mapping through both the homepage and reports page, and we have had more than fifteen million viewers globally on these pages. IPAB has been featured several times across many media groups both nationally and internationally, such as *New York Times*, BBC News, *Times of India*, *Deccan Chronicle*, as well as many others. Our research and findings have been quoted by the World Bank, United Nations, as well as Transparency International. Harvard Business School and London School of Economics have cited us in their curriculum. Across India, we have been called for as many as ten educational programs and six national level conferences.[7]

The website data is based on inputs from the predominantly urban populace who have access to digital media such as phones, computers, etc. Thus, the rural sectors are not well represented. However, in India we are witnessing a phenomenon by which the Internet has become a hub for mass movements against corruption, which otherwise cannot be done on the ground. We have been at the forefront of this phenomenon because we provide an easy space for citizens to report their stories and experiences regarding corruption. However, with our only-online presence currently, we do realise that we can only touch people who have access to the Internet, who are in a minority. However, this number is likely to grow rapidly in India, therefore, our influence is likely to spread even more.

Activism, whether on the streets or online, has to have substance and be sustained. Ranting or venting anger is not enough. Protests, such as processions, can momentarily draw attention, but any effort at a change must be sustained in order to translate it into action. The key is to work on systemic reform and then advocate the government to accept and implement specific suggestions to reduce corruption. Providing a forum for citizens to report their experiences is only the beginning of a long journey. We aim to achieve a measurable increase in the number of people who resist corruption, as also in the number of processes within the government that we have been able to change for the better. That is what IPAB measures as a success. Some examples of such stories are shared here.

Registering a property and paying bribe has become synonymous in many parts of our country. So much so, that the bribe is now re-termed fancily as 'facilitation fee', and many think it is mandatory to shell out this amount to get their houses registered. While many don't mind bribing to get their works done quickly, Bengaluru resident Vyjayanthi Mala sets an example by not only refusing to grease palms but also going against the tide to get her home registered the right way.[8]

Deepanshu Garg was duped by an employee of an Aadhaar enrolment centre in Pune into paying a registration fee for enrolling for the card. When he realised that he had been tricked, he highlighted the issue on IPAB. The outreach team of IPAB immediately forwarded the complaint to the UID vigilance and director's office. In February, Deepanshu received a call from the UID vigilance office informing him that the Aadhaar enrolment centre has been blacklisted and an investigation has been initiated.[9]

As digital literacy increases and more people interact in larger numbers with the government, they will demand services over the Internet, as also report and give their feedback on the government over it. Both politicians and officials cannot ignore the influence the Internet will have on democracy in the coming years.

Dissemination

IPAB seeks to utilise the mapped information in advocacy measures on the ground as well as in framing policies in research projects. To elaborate, the data sourced from our website is actively screened weekly by our senior advisors—Malati Das and S.T. Ramesh. Janaagraha certainly does not have any statutory or enforcement powers when addressing the issue of 'retail' corruption (that is, corruption experienced by citizens on a day-to-day basis when availing public services); therefore, we forward these complaints to the relevant departments with the expectation that (a) they will be treated as citizens' grievances and (b) we will receive an endorsement regarding the action taken. These action taken reports are posted on the website with the potential to create a favourable impression of the department's responsiveness to grievances.

In one such instance, a Nandini Milk parlour in Jayanagar in Bengaluru (a franchise of Karnataka Cooperative Milk Producers Federation Ltd.) charged Rs 2 more than the maximum retail price per milk packet. While Rs 2 is a negligible amount, the parlour had a footfall of over 500 people. One can calculate the amount of profit the shop owner may have made illegally. The grievance posted by a customer on IPAB was immediately brought to the attention of Malati Das, who is also an advisor at IPAB. She forwarded the complaint to Karnataka Cooperative Milk Producers Federation Ltd. in Bengaluru. The cooperative issued a notice to the owner of the Nandini franchise, stating that selling Nandini products at more than the MRP violated the contract, and issued a warning.[10]

Unfortunately, the response from certain departments like stamps and registration, police, Bruhat Bengaluru Mahanagara Palike (BBMP) has not been as encouraging. When addressed with an issue of corruption, correspondence tends to go unanswered, or the complaint is bounced around from department to department and never resolved. It would be helpful if the departments could deal with these complaints promptly as per rules and keep IPAB informed of the action taken so that this information can be posted on our website. If the government can issue a circular to the effect that grievances forwarded by IPAB must be treated on par with grievances submitted directly by individuals, and redressal should be prompt and IPAB must be duly informed of the disposal of grievances, then the government's drive to reduce corruption would be supplemented by our endeavours.

Through online initiatives we can collect actual corruption reports from the people, which in turn will help us use the same as a collective, to propose policy changes/action. The functioning of offline and online functions are equally important. Jana Mahiti (People's Information) Reports are a research and advocacy initiative based on citizens' reports on IPAB. We analyse the procedures and processes of specific departments with reference to the patterns of corruption reported by citizens and suggest how processual reforms can be introduced to eliminate corruption. The Jana Mahitis also contain citizen-friendly information about Acts, rules and procedures, as information is empowering and enables resistance to corruption. IPAB has brought out Jana Mahiti Reports on the department of transport (2011), stamps and registration (2011) and police verification of passport (2016). A new report on processual reform of the procedures relating to the sale of immovable property in the department of tamps and registration was published in April 2017.

We seek the assistance of the government in two ways:

1. The departments may take cognizance of the Jana Mahiti Reports and act on the recommendations where feasible.
2. The departments could identify areas that are vulnerable to corruption, thereby requiring processual reform, and ask IPAB to prepare a Jana Mahiti in consultation with the departments.

A study of 'Jana Mahiti Report 2016' by Janaagraha Centre for Citizenship and Democracy revealed that the police verification process emerged as one of the biggest sources of corruption and harassment of new passport applicants in the entire process.[11] S.T. Ramesh, a former state police chief, who put together the report, said they analysed 1,149 crowdsourced complaints from the website—ipaidabribe.com—related to police verification between 2010 and 2014. The analysis showed that Rs 38.71 lakh was paid as bribe.

Soon after the report came out, plans to develop a passport verification app that simplifies the entire process was announced by the government. In the year 2018, the Ministry of External Affairs launched the mPassport Seva app, which has made the procedure for applying for a passport and its verification much easier.

Immediate and Long-term Implications

IPAB is looking forward to increasing engagement with the Government of India in the near future. The senior advisors along with the IPAB team met with the chief secretary of Karnataka in April 2017 to discuss the same. IPAB believes that the process of grievance redressal can be improved by having a robust follow-up process, which can improve the response rate from government agencies for bribe related complaints. This will, in turn, catalyse departmental inquiries/action against corrupt officers, thus strongly dis-incentivising corruption. Similarly, if the government implements a few of the recommendations made in the processual reform reports, it will help in reducing bribery, as well as legislative and institutional loopholes leading to it, thus increasing transparency and ensuring good governance. Finally, if the government can assist IPAB by empanelling educational institutions for outreach workshops based on the present model, as well as incorporate studies on fighting corruption in their curriculum, then the knowledge dissemination will cause greater impact.

Strategizing on long-term goals, IPAB would like to collaborate with international partner nations to research country-specific bribe trends for aiding governance. Education and best-practice sharing between IPAB India and international partners, through studies, conferences, seminars etc. IPaidABribe envisions improved mapping and data visualisation in the future, by collaborating with Information technology and market research firms, which can help in better knowledge sharing and policy analysis of government public service delivery across India. Reaching out and encouraging citizens—to report even the smallest bribe amounts, to find all loopholes and analyse gaps across public policies and services leading to institutional and administrative reform—is paramount to our vision. Finally, IPAB seeks to build a website and an app with a new and improved user interface.

Conclusion

Our intent is to change the system that creates corruption, rather than indict individuals within the system. Besides, even if you change the individuals, the threat of corruption remains. But changing the system will root out corruption permanently.

The role that non-government bodies play is multi-fold since corruption is such a vast and hydra-headed monster. From procurement processes in public projects to extraction of precious natural resources to public services and favouritism/nepotism towards private enterprises, everything is rife with corruption and everything can be used as instruments for wealth and/or power.

Just as governments introduce critical vigilance bodies, integrity offices, ethics departments, etc. to curb corruption, non-government bodies play an equally important role in providing independent platforms to amplify the voice and experience of citizens and to catalyse change.

Crowdsourcing has been adopted as a strategy to build large databases, but not for assessing the quality of government services. The more hits we get, the greater the influence of the site on governance and policy. As of today, the Internet is still a minor influence on the government. This, however, is bound to change. As younger people who are more conversant with the Internet interact in larger numbers with the government, they will demand better services, and also report and give their feedback on governments and governance online. Both politicians and officials can no longer ignore the influence the Internet will have on democracy in the coming years.

Notes

1. These include everything from airports, banking, customs, immigration, education, infrastructure, tax, judiciary, social welfare, passports and so on. A total of thirty-five such categories exist in the form.
2. Link to the video: https://www.youtube.com/watch?v=RQ3-82CfUow
3. Report and video: http://www.ipaidabribe.com/champions/meet-bribe-fighting-software-engineer#gsc.tab=0

4. Mujhse Hogi Shuruvaat video. The song was sung by India's prominent singer Shankar Mahadevan. It was also nominated for Honesty Oscar Award 2014 under the Best Original Song category. https://www.youtube.com/watch?v=a3dlOroKJXo
5. The full report is available here: http://www.janaagraha.org/files/publications/CRBI.pdf
6. Countries we have partnered with: http://ipaidabribe.com/partners#gsc.tab=0
7. An example of one such collaboration is the inaugural edition of the Coalition Against Corruption (CoCo) conference, co-hosted by Janaagraha. See http://janaagraha.org/files/CoCo-Report-Final-2014.pdf
8. http://ipaidabribe.com/champions/bengalurean-goes-against-the-tide-to-register-property-without-bribe#gsc.tab=0
9. http://ipaidabribe.com/champions/techie-gets-corrupt-aadhaar-enrolment-centre-blacklisted#gsc.tab=0
10. Link to the action report: http://ipaidabribe.com/champions/bengalureans-complaint-on-ipaidabribe-results-in-a-warning-to-a-jayanagar-nandini-milk-parlour-1#gsc.tab=0
11. https://www.thehindu.com/news/cities/bangalore/police-verification-a-big-source-of-corruption-study/article8520334.ece

10

STREETS AND CIVIC PARTICIPATION (FixMyStreet)

Interview with Rebecca Rumbul, by Nooreen Reza

FixMyStreet (FMS) is an interactive mapping platform created by MySociety, a not-for-profit enterprise focused on increasing civic participation to foster healthy democracies. FMS was designed for users to report problems in their neighbourhoods, that then gets routed through the site to the attention of their local councils. From 2007 to 2017, more than 1.1 million user reports about local issues were submitted to council authorities via FixMyStreet (Matthews et al. 2018). The usefulness of a citizen-driven project like FMS has been highlighted as austerity measures and budget cuts in the UK have reduced the funding available to councils to do their own investigations into neighbourhoods' needs (Matthews et al. 2018).

However, as the makers of FixMyStreet have learned over the many years of administering the platform, different communities have varying levels of access to and usage of the site. Data collected from eleven years of the map's existence showed wealthier areas submitting more reports than more deprived neighbourhoods over time. Interestingly, the patterns of complaints lodged also fall into different categories depending on the broader socio-economic makeup of the neighbourhoods from which users are reporting (Matthews et al. 2018). In addition, according to a 2015 research report, while 9 per cent of the UK's population identified as a non-white ethnic minority in the 2011 census, 94 per cent of FMS's users were white (Rumbul 2015, 11). Despite these real challenges in expanding the use of the platform to those whose needs and environmental problems are underrepresented, MySociety remains hopeful and determined that FixMyStreet can be an effective form of 'civic technology', an online tool citizens can use to push their governments to be more transparent and accountable to the public (Rumbul 2015, 2).

In late 2017, I spoke with Rebecca Rumbul, head of research at MySociety, whose role is to engage in experiments and qualitative research to look at how MySociety's technology, and civic technology more broadly, is changing people and institutions. We spoke about FixMyStreet's origins and development, its everyday functioning challenges and the team's hopes for its future as a tool of civic engagement. This interview has been edited for clarity.

Can you tell us about the origins of FixMyStreet? Who was involved? Was there a precipitating event that made you all want to make the platform?

There wasn't one specific event that our team at the time looked at and thought, 'Oh my god, we need to do something in relation to X'. We think that most of this kind of civic tech is borne of general frustrations in ordinary life, and I don't think FMS was any different. At the time we were a very small team. It was before I joined. We had a group of extremely talented developers, who had a lot of side projects, and a lot of ideas for projects they would like to do. Back then there wasn't an enormous amount of funding available for this kind of project. So, it was something that was kind of on the sidelines—like 'we'd like to create something around this concept'—for a while.

Then we developed a partnership with the Young Foundation.[1] We were able to get some funding from the Department of Constitutional Affairs' Innovation Fund,[2] to actually bring this kind of vision to life. It actually didn't start life as FixMyStreet; it started life as 'Neighbourhood Fix It', which launched in February of 2007. It was the same concept as it is now, just to generally assist users in reporting incidents of broken civic infrastructure. So it was really meant to be a kind of forum where users can take part in discussions about maintaining and improving the infrastructure and environment of the neighbourhood.

I think, even though it's always been an issue-reporting site, there was always the hope that it would enable people to discuss more positive improvements or things they like to see, instead of just identifying issues. We haven't actually really grown into that kind of platform yet, just because we're not sure how it would work, in terms of from the authority [council] side of things. So, there wasn't really anything specific; it was just generally, 'We can do this, we think we can do it well, and we need the funding to go and do it'.

Did that early iteration, Neighbourhood Fix It, also have the reporting mechanism where you would submit incidents to the municipal councils or was it just more of a platform to make the information publicly available?
No, it was pretty much as it is now, just a 2007 version (laughs). So a little bit more clunky, not quite as sexy. It was pretty much as it is now, just, you know, a beta version. It was renamed FixMyStreet only six months later actually when the domain name became available (laughs).

So the idea, or the hope you had behind it, was to build civic participation on a really local level?
Yeah, our thinking behind it was, actually, people know far better what's broken in the neighbourhood than people in the council offices know. Residents have a far better understanding of when something is broken, when something needs fixing, whatever. Instead of them having to figure out how to contact their councils and ask for that to be fixed—because a lot of the time that would've been dealt with in council customer service centres—they could just use the new tech available to report it fairly seamlessly.

So it was really very much about just putting power in the hands of citizens, being able to say, 'Look you know this is broken; you need to fix it, it's your responsibility', rather than a person trying to hunt out an e-mail address or phone number and then go through the effort of actually writing an e-mail or phoning somebody; and then being on the phone with somebody, trying to describe the issue, trying to describe where it is and then putting the phone down and never knowing if someone is actually going to do anything.

So the traditional ways of contacting your council have basically just been to hunt down individual e-mails or a general hotline, or something much less streamlined?
Oh yeah, it's similar over here to how it is in the United States. In the past, it's just been a horrible experience trying to get your local authority to do anything or to know who to talk to in the bureaucratic silos.

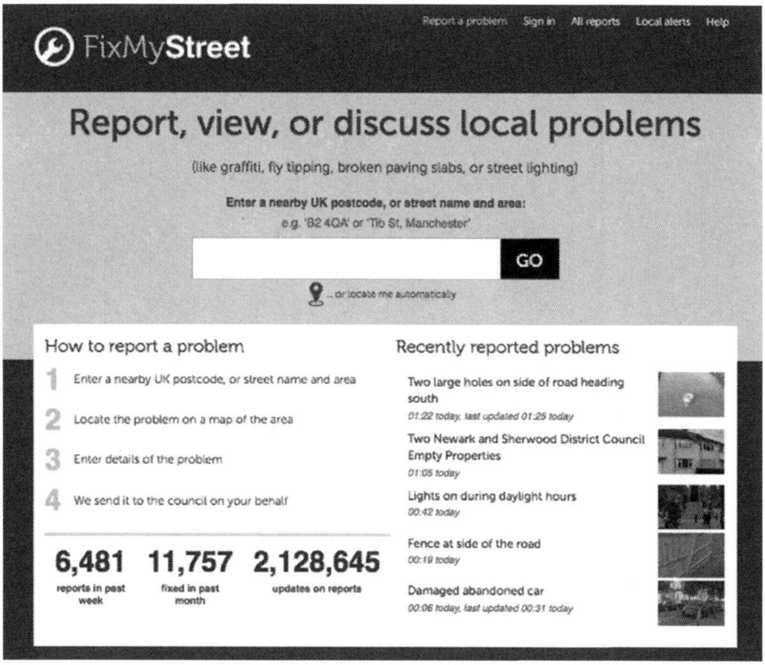

Figure 10.1: FixMyStreet (UK) homepage.
Source: FixMyStreet website.

We're also interested in hearing about the specific design choices that were made when you were developing the map. Can you tell us about the process of designing the site and if there were certain parts of it that the team wanted to make sure were highlighted or more visible for some reason—whether that reason was aesthetic or they thought it would increase usership, or anything else?

We had some really wonderful designers on the team who, when they came in, had a look at the site and said: (a) let's try to make it prettier and (b) let's try to make it more user-friendly. The two core things we try to do with all of our sites is to make sure they're as short and seamless as possible, from landing on the site to being able to finish your transaction. So that's why the front page is fairly simple (see Figure 10.1). The first thing is, we're primarily assuming you're coming on the site to do what the site does, which is report an issue, and including the address where you are. Obviously, now we can locate you automatically, so now a user can just go to the point of interest where something is broken. That is always a significant design decision, the question of how we can make this as easy as possible for the actual, normal user.

In terms of the trackers, like how many reports in the past week were fixed, updates, that kind of thing, we also think it's important to provide a bit of a feedback loop. With FMS, councils are under no obligation to actually go on the website and mark something as fixed. So we do go on the site and automatically ask users after about two weeks. We contact them and say, 'Has it been fixed?' I think we'll contact them once again, like in a couple of months' time, and ask them to mark it as fixed because that helps with the tune-up of the site. We basically want to show as much as possible that there is a feedback loop and that we can close that cycle of people making reports and stuff actually getting fixed.

So it's great. We want to show that people are using the site and are making reports, but really, one of the most important things for us is making sure that reports are being fixed. We're very, very concerned with doing research on how our sites like this are working because at the end of the day we don't just want people to be able to report problems. We see this as doing something civic; we see this as contributing to people's civic involvement. People will be civically engaged while they believe that someone is actually listening and someone is actually doing something. People will probably quickly lose interest in using a site like this if nothing is ever fixed. So we make sure that we do research as well, to make sure that this assumption is actually true.

Do you have trouble getting users to respond to inquiries about things if they have been fixed, or are people generally eager to update the site?

It's a bit of both. There are always people that are not going to have time to come back on the site and say, 'Yes it was fixed'. We hope that the little reminder jogs people into doing it, but they don't have to. We're certainly not in the business of just keeping on prodding people because that's not going to make them anymore engaged, either. I think generally people do mark things as fixed, and councils can, too. Ideally, it would be good if we had 100 per cent of users marking things as fixed, or saying, 'No this is still broken'.

It may be difficult to give a quantitative answer to this, but do you feel like more people respond when things are still broken or when they're fixed?
I would say most people respond when things have been fixed. We get a lot of both, but, generally, just because of the way we phrase the e-mail, it's more a case of, 'Let us know if it's fixed, because if it's not fixed the pin will stay up there [on the map]'. The report is still with the authority, so there's not a lot of point in saying that it's still broken. Whereas what we really want is for people to tell us if and when it's been fixed.

Contacting people and asking them if something has been fixed is a form of content moderation in itself and monitoring the site from the developer's end. Are there other ways where you have to engage in that kind of moderation?
We have a user policy where we reserve the right to remove things that are not helpful, or not within the usage guidelines of the site. We allow comments to be made on certain issues that have been pinned, so we do have to moderate that somewhat. To be honest, we don't get an awful lot of issues with this—a lot of the stuff is just not controversial (laughs). If there's a pothole there's a pothole! It's either there or it's not. Every now and again someone will get a bit overexcited, and we will have to take certain things down or make sure certain people aren't clogging up the map or doing anything like that, but luckily it's not a big issue.

Do you have issues with people reporting the same thing over and over?
Not mostly, because if someone has already reported it, then the pin will be on the map for everyone to see. So it's actually quite difficult to put multiple reports of the same things on the map. If you're clicking on the map, and somebody's already reported it, then you're just clicking on the pin that's already there.

So with the map itself, you can't just put a pin in the same place again?
No, if there's a pin that's existing, then we also advise people that if there is a pin that's already there, then there is not much point in reporting it again. Unless, you know, it's been years and years and years and it's still

broken. If it's an issue that has been reported in the last week or so there's really not that much point in reporting it again.

You mentioned some earlier challenges with funding the site. Can you talk about some additional issues you faced in the process of creating the site or trying to promote user engagement? If you found that certain things were not working with your original approach, what changes did you make to try and make the site more user friendly or more effective?

I think one of the biggest challenges when it first launched was making sure councils themselves were amenable to it. You know, 2007, that was 10 years ago. Most people weren't even on Facebook in 2007. So with this kind of quite new, disruptive service, some councils thought, 'Whoa, what's going on here, I don't understand this, getting these automated e-mails from this service'. At first, there were quite a few councils that said, 'You know what, we're not going to accept anything that comes from the site'. So we had to make sure that the people using the site in those areas where the council refused to accept a report were aware of that.

So, what we recognised was that we couldn't build a site that was just good for users and easy for users alone. We had to improve the site and how we present it so that it works for local authorities as well. We had to do a bit of, not peacemaking, but explaining to local authorities. FMS for them was, in some instances, so new that they didn't really know how to handle it, and like I said, some authorities just immediately clammed up and said, 'We can't engage with this'.

A few others, once we explained that it's just the same as someone sending you an e-mail and it's going to the same customer inbox as if you were to send someone at the council an e-mail directly, and so it shouldn't be any different, then a lot of councils were fine with that. But because of the age of a lot of council systems over here, the way IT used to be procured in local government was very, very cumbersome, very clunky. A lot of councils found themselves receiving these reports and having to get someone else to type them all back into their own database anyway. So they were saying, 'Well, this is creating work for us'.

Those kinds of issues are evolution issues. They're issues with tech on the outside moving faster than tech on the inside of institutions. Slowly over the years, it's gotten better and better, to where we are now when we have actually created FixMyStreet Pro for councils, so they have a back end that this plugs straight into and that manages their maintenance workflows. It almost bypasses the customer service lines completely, and it just goes straight to the department where it's needed. So with those teething issues, there was a recognition that with this kind of civic tech to get better at closing feedback loops and to get citizens a better service, we need to be working inside the government as well as on the outside (see Figure 10.2).

Figure 10.2: FixMyStreet map with user reports, showing the city of Cambridge, UK.
Source: FixMyStreet website.

Would you say that you have pretty good coverage ten years later in terms of councils that accept reports from the site?
Oh yeah, these days I think there might be one council that still doesn't accept reports, but every other one is fine now.

When did FixMyStreet Pro come out?
I don't actually know when it formally came out. We started developing it a couple of years back, and it's now operating in about five or six councils in the UK. I don't know what stage of deployment they are at yet, but I think that there are six councils that are clients. Obviously, that is not nearly as many as we would like since there are over a hundred

councils in the UK. Still, it's slowly going the right way. Even councils that we aren't selling FMS Pro to, we've still been consulting with things like Open311, which again will help them not just with FMS but with other kinds of tools that are being built like this.

So, that example I just gave you about how we are trying to change institutions from the inside, this piece of civic tech has shown councils that they need to change their internal procedures, and as such teeny tiny little websites like this are actually pushing councils into the 21st century a little bit more.

Going back to this question of surprises and things you didn't expect in the process of data collection. In some ways, like you said, it's not very controversial to report a pothole or report issues. So you wouldn't think there would be issues with neutrality or bias in the system itself. But have you had conversations about that if there are ways in which the map facilitates over-reporting or under-reporting of certain things?

One of the main things we are worried about is the user base, and we have done some research into this. What we are concerned about is, 'Are only people in wealthy areas reporting, and is that distorting how councils are actually doing maintenance?' We'd hate to think that this kind of platform, which we'd like to think would democratise issue reporting, was actually only helping people that were already pretty good at this kind of thing anyway.

We have looked at our user base, and it is not really representative of local populations from what we can tell from the figures. It is generally a more male-dominated reporting user base; they tend to be older and tend to be in wealthier areas. This is something that we are concerned with and that we are looking at. We don't know if a consequence of that is that a council will actually focus more of their efforts on maintaining very wealthy areas to the detriment of poorer areas. So we have been experimenting with the design of the site, the language we use and the visual imagery we use. We're trying to experiment to make sure women are equally reporting issues, and that people in less advantaged areas are reporting issues.

Looking at our user base, it's not too bad overall; we were worried that there would be a distortion [for councils] but there's actually not.

We're also using other external databases to overlap with the data we've got on FMS to look at whether things like internet speeds or access are an issue in terms of where there are more or fewer reports. So user base is something that we're very fixated on and making sure that it's not having any kind of detrimental effect anywhere.

On a related point, how did you publicise the platform? Have you been trying to spread the word by using different kinds of methods to reach people that your research is showing are not using it in the same numbers yet?

Definitely. Over the years, we have tried as much as possible to publicise the platform. It's very difficult when you're a charity. Communications and publicity are the last things on the long list of items we like doing, but we do have a communications manager that promotes it as much as possible. It's on Facebook and Twitter and that kind of stuff. Everything is on Github as well, so there's a big developer community that knows about it. People also discover it through councils, just by the fact that this is a service they are familiar with. Some councils have even paid us to integrate FMS on their own council websites now, which is great.

We try and plug it as much as possible. Every now and then we will do leaflets in libraries and that kind of thing, and making sure that people like the Good Things Foundation and Citizens Advice Bureaus know about us and they can tell people as well. It's always an uphill struggle trying to make sure that people know that this service is out there.

Can you talk a little bit more about your social media presence?

There's not a lot to tell. We've got Facebook pages and Twitter feeds. We don't do anywhere near as much on those feeds as other organisations do. We're very, very British in that we try not to bother people too much. The kind of services we provide is such that we want to be there for people when they need us. Because we are trying to enable people to do something civic, that not only benefits them but also benefits their community; we try not to lay it on too thick for fear of scaring people off or annoying people. We try to be present but not overpowering.

Is there a hypothetical point you reach in terms of user participation where you feel like you've kind of reached your potential with FMS? Or is there never really a point where it would be like—there's enough people reporting?

I certainly wouldn't think we are anywhere close to that yet. There are an awful lot of people that don't know about FMS and, therefore, aren't using it. I think it would be a very, very long time before we said, you know we're done.

The rollout of FMS Pro for councils will make sure that the site continues to be useful even if people aren't necessarily on the site; if we have implemented it on a council website then that is still being useful. The code is also open-source, so it's running all over the world. It's something that we really believe is worthy of support and our continued attention.

The code is also very adaptable, so we've used it for a different site called Collideoscope, which is pretty much exactly the same. But the purpose of that site is to report where cyclists have had near misses, so where they have almost had an accident but have not, or had a minor accident. We encourage them to use this service to report those things so that, hopefully, we can identify places where someone might get killed. If there are enough incidents clustered in one area, for instance, the council can look it up and say, 'It's only a matter of time before someone is seriously injured here, so we need to do something about this'.

The code's also being used for things like disaster zones where buildings are unsafe. So we've got this incredibly flexible open-source code that can be employed for all sorts of uses. Obviously, FMS is ours and it's the initial thing, so we all continue to support it as long as we can. One of the other reasons we developed FMS Pro was to make it more sustainable to keep supporting FMS as a free service.

Like you said, you want to keep supporting FMS into the foreseeable future. Are there any specific visions or goals you have for the platform itself going forward?

Nothing above what we have made public. We are focusing on FMS Pro at the moment, which we hope will be a really useful and viable resource for councils. But you have to remember we don't get any funding from anywhere to run FMS. It's supported by our other work, so we really don't have an enormous amount of capacity to devote to thinking about ways to change it or take it forward as such. If we manage to use FMS Pro, and if it is picked up by more councils that are willing to pay for that service, then that will support FMS and perhaps give us the capacity to do other things with it.

As you mentioned, there are other FMS platforms in other countries. Are those up and running now? Have the teams working on those other platforms reached out to you?
Some of them do, some of them don't! There's one in Malaysia, there's a couple in Latin America. Some organisations around the world will reach out to us and say, 'We really want to deploy this, will you come and help us?' If we've got the money to do so, then we will. The most successful spin-off outside of the UK is in Norway. We know who they are, but we don't interact with them much because they are very techie people and don't really need our assistance. If we get time and funding in the future, we would really like to do some kind of comparative research about the uses of the platform in other countries.

Obviously, the code is out there, so if you have the code you can just pick it up and use it yourself. We've actually had a couple of instances where people have tried to pick the code up and tried to sell it, which wasn't great! Again, it's open-source so we don't want to impose ourselves on any group, but we do try to develop some kind of relationship with them so that we know how it's being used and how it is going.

Notes

1. The Young Foundation is a not-for-profit research foundation and social investor that supports community development initiatives. https://youngfoundation.org/about-us/
2. Now part of the Ministry of Justice. https://www.gov.uk/government/organisations/department-for-constitutional-affairs

References

Matthews, P., A. Rae, E. Nyanzu and A. Parsons. *FixMyStreet! The Geography of Citizen Reporting on Neighbourhood Issues in the UK*. [online] mySociety Research, 2018. https://research.mysociety.org/media/outputs/fixmystreet-geography-of-citizen-reporting1.1.pdf (accessed on 2 June 2020).

Rumbul, Rebecca. *Who Benefits from Civic Technology? Demographic and Public Attitudes Research into the Users of Civic Technologies.* [online] mySociety Research, 2015. https://research.mysociety.org/media/outputs/demographics-report.pdf (accessed on 2 June 2020).

AFTERWORD
Methods and Social Impacts of Mapping the World Today

Shannon Mattern

The world has witnessed a rich variety of cartographic traditions and place-marking practices over the millennia. From sky charts painted on cave walls to a map of the world—or what was then known of it—meticulously squeezed onto a small clay tablet, these pre-Common Era proto-maps didn't likely lend themselves to the involvement of multiple hands. While the spatial knowledge they embodied was undoubtedly the product of a collective intelligence evolved over the ages, the actual cartographic mark-making couldn't have been a widely communal affair.

Ptolemy's lines of latitude and longitude eventually enveloped the globe in a universalising grid, and that universalism readily lent itself to imperialist ends as cartographers, aided by star catalogues and astrolabes, created for their states and mercantile sponsors new maps of an ever-expanding known world. The following millennia brought sextants and geographic information systems and satellite imagery—tools that, for the most part, kept cartography and spatial ontologies and epistemologies in the hands of a powerful, privileged few.

Yet the rise of digital mapping tools—from consumer GPS devices to Google Maps and Open Street Map—has famously opened up cartography to a wider public. For that expanding cartographic community, maps have become an everyday presence—customised and pocket-sized. And, more importantly, the wider public now has the capacity to make their own maps, chronicle their own spatial experiences and model their own worlds. Those marginalised populations who had historically been only cartographic *subjects*—'native' populations of colonised territories, recipients of aid from global development organisations, 'redlined' communities and other inhabitants of the margins—now wield the digital sextant. Women, people of colour, the impecunious and other victims of both historical and contemporary injustices can plot their individual and collective lived experiences and validate their own ways of knowing, data that are often of little value to commercial cartographic interests. And through this auto-cartography, as Siddharth Peter de Souza, Nida Rehman and Saba Sharma explain in their introduction to this volume, 'these populations can potentially hold governments accountable … fill gaps when infrastructural and municipal services are fragmented … call attention to a variety of issues that impact everyday lives such as sexual or political violence, environmental injustice, or corruption, and … make visible social and political processes and events that might be otherwise hidden or overlooked.'

There is much to celebrate in these developments. And many other scholars, activists, policymakers, global aid workers, development organisations and citizen cartographers have indeed cheered the democratisation and radicalisation of cartography for the past few decades. Yet what sets deSouza, Rehman and Sharma's *Crowdsourcing, Constructing and Collaborating* apart is its choice to give voice to the mapmakers themselves, to afford them an opportunity to discuss their motivations and development processes, to celebrate their successes and to reflect on their challenges. We are at a point now in the history of participatory GIS and crowdsourced mapping when we *can* reflect critically on such projects: the ambiguity or ambition of their initial goals, the constraints of available tools and the limitations of their reach and impact. As most of the mapmakers featured in this volume productively acknowledge, maps alone are rarely sufficient to achieve social and environmental change, to affect policy reform or to incite political revolution. Instead, crowdsourced, collaborative mapping—revolutionary as it may have been at its inception—is best framed as merely one tool, albeit a critical one, for rallying local and global communities, for lobbying politicians, for deploying resources on the ground and inciting the exchange of embodied skills and knowledge.

What's more, if it is to have 'social impacts' as implied by the book's subtitle, digital mapping has to be conceived as just as much analogue and embedded as it is virtual and distributed. This is particularly true for cartographic 'content', the data that populate the map. As we see in 'Placing Segregation' and 'Palestine Open Map', building a robust digital map is not merely a matter of downloading the right comprehensive dataset. Instead, representing marginalised populations or obscured spatial histories requires the laborious, meticulous synthesis of myriad archival sources and the cross-referencing and normalisation of their metadata and data models. Streets and neighbourhoods have different names from one century to the next. Censuses adopt different protocols and different means of determining who gets to count as a human subject—a whole, sovereign individual. Cartographers and their collaborative partners have devised methods for reconciling these disparate categories while not glossing over the historical legacies of bias.

Most platforms draw on an array of living data sources. For HarassMap and I Paid a Bribe, cartographic data comprise human experiences—affectively charged, often painful and humiliating encounters. FixMyStreet registers self-reported 'glitches' in the physical environment and, ideally, their eventual repair. And Humanitarian Tracker and Missing Maps both require empirical work: volunteer cartographers put their bodies on the line to report disasters and create field maps in conflict zones and treacherous, remote terrains.

Cartographers' bodies are also summoned for less precarious labour. Mapathons are a common means of generating data for and building communities around these mapping platforms. Intolerance Tracker, Palestine Open Maps and Missing Maps gather volunteer mappers at social events where they geo-rectify base maps, extract data from satellite images and turn analogue materials into machine-readable resources. Quality control and verification—responsibilities that can, in some cases, be distributed to a volunteer team, or, in others, might be left to a core leadership group—likewise require sufficient human engagement. As Missing Maps' Jan Böhm explains, mapathons also serve as a means of sustaining the cartographic community, establishing a pathway of succession as one group steps away from the project and another moves in to take its place. The labour of digital upkeep—and the burnout it effects—is one of the key analogue concerns for crowdsourced mapping projects and of open-source technology projects in general.

Yet even a robustly populated, quality-checked map isn't enough to stand on its own. Many platform leaders find it necessary, and greatly rewarding, to engage in community outreach to help local residents and officials both appreciate the value of their maps and the value of their platforms' larger social missions. I Paid a Bribe and FixMyStreet regularly liaise with local government officials to ensure that they're attending to and acting on contributors' reports of corruption and disrepair. IPAB, likewise, uses its platform as a means of educating users about basic government services. Intolerance Tracker's and FemMap's leaders, in seeking to create international or global resource-sharing networks, have laboured to convince other like-minded outlets of the value of building global alliances. HarassMap's stewards, meanwhile, have sought to turn *bystanders*—witnesses to sexual harassment—into allies:

> Using the map and reports to convince people to take the issue [of harassment] seriously and challenge stereotypes that served as excuses, volunteers from all Egypt's governorates worked within their own neighbourhoods to attract agents of change who are willing to shift their behaviour, in hopes of reaching a 'tipping point' and affect a wider crowd.

'Community Captains', equipped with insights from the map, lead volunteer teams on 'outreach days', where they incite public conversations about harassment and encourage bystander intervention. They also created a Safe Areas program through which shopkeepers and Uber drivers and other businesses and institutions can display their commitment to anti-harassment.

In order to transform the realities reflected on their maps—worlds rife with oppression, corruption and injustice—many of these cartographers use their collaborative platforms as tools for embodied, street-level activism. Yet many of these same mapmakers also lament the significant rifts and tensions between the spatial ontologies and ideologies embedded in the dominant mapping software, to which they are beholden, and the safer and more just worlds they hope to create. What are the political implications of relying on Google Maps and software like ArcGis, with their seeming neutrality and authority as well as naturalised cartographic conventions like the Mercator projection and North-up orientation, or interfaces that privilege English-language interaction?

While these platforms and protocols are widely legible and relatively user-friendly—and while their ubiquity enhances their cultural capital and interoperability—their embedded epistemologies and politics contradict the emancipatory missions that *Crowdsourcing*'s authors embrace. As deSouza, Rehman, Sharma and Nooren Reza write in this volume, Google Maps and similar tools tend to 'reify and naturalise boundaries and hegemonic delineations of territory while obscuring a myriad of contestations and claims'. Among those contestations are place names and borders in colonised territories and conflict zones, and local, indigenous traditions for denoting location or representing presence, all of which embody diverse spatial ontologies and land claims, and most of which are then reduced to a standard universalised mode of representation on a digital map. A traumatising assault, a casualty of war, a frustrating interaction with a corrupt bureaucrat, a pothole that grows wider by the week, all become a point on a map, localised at a particular address or intersection, despite the fact that the effects of these interactions and the systems that make them possible extend across the globe.

These digital maps, revolutionary in some regards and hegemonic and colonialist in others, are merely tools in a larger enterprise. Crowdsourced mapping has reached a stage of maturity when we can accept, as the authors in this volume do, that they are not ends in themselves. Rather, they're our digital astrolabes or sextants, indexing local embodied knowledge and global patterns, connecting stakeholders and allies as they collaboratively remake the worlds they're mapping.

INDEX

Note: The letter 'n' following locators refers to notes.

W

Y

ABOUT THE EDITORS AND CONTRIBUTORS

Editors

Siddharth Peter de Souza is a PhD candidate at Humboldt University of Berlin. His research is related to understanding the politics behind the development of legal indicators and their impacts as tools of global governance. Siddharth is the founder of Justice Adda and a co-founder of Intolerance Tracker, and previously worked as a German Chancellor Fellow at the Max Planck Foundation for Peace and Rule of Law in Heidelberg and as a judicial clerk at the High Court of Delhi.

Nida Rehman is the Lucian and Rita Caste Assistant Professor at the School of Architecture, Carnegie Mellon University, Pittsburgh, Pennsylvania, and recently completed her PhD in the Department of Geography at the University of Cambridge. She is a co-founder of Intolerance Tracker. Her work looks at the ecological, political and historical dimensions of urban environmental change, particularly in South Asia.

Saba Sharma is a co-founder of Intolerance Tracker and has recently completed her PhD from the Department of Geography, University of Cambridge. She previously worked at the Centre for Equity Studies, New Delhi.

Contributors

Ahmad Barclay is an architect and environmental designer presently based in Beirut. He is a co-founder of arenaofspeculation.org and also works on Visualizing Palestine and #3awda. Ahmad previously worked with Decolonizing Architecture Art Residency (DAAR) on the Laboratory of Returns project, investigating architectural models for the return of Palestinian refugees.

Angie Abdelmonem has a PhD in anthropology. She is a US National Science Foundation postdoctoral research fellow and a faculty associate at Arizona State University. Her research centres on sexual violence and social movements in Egypt and the Middle East. She has served as a consultant for HarassMap.

Daniela Del Bene is a postdoctoral researcher at the Institute of Environmental Science and Technology (ICTA), Autonomous University of Barcelona, Catalunya, Spain. Her work mainly focuses on water resources, dams and hydropower projects, energy sovereignty and socio-ecological transformations. She is the main editor and coordinator of the EJAtlas.

Dheeman Ghosh is a development sector professional with about a decade of experience in education, skill development, good governance and sustainability. He served as a senior associate at Civic Participation, Janaagraha Centre for Citizenship and Democracy.

Farah Shash is a Community Psychologist working in the fields of Human Rights and Community Development, specialised in issues of gender and sexual and gender-based violence. She is currently the Chair of HarassMap, a volunteer-based organisation working to end sexual harassment in Egypt.

Hend Alhinnawi, while working and travelling through the Middle East and Africa, was inspired by ordinary people doing extraordinary things. She is the founder and CEO of Humanitarian Tracker, a global non-profit that uses crowdsourcing and artificial intelligence for the public good. Hend has worked with the World Health Organization, World Food Program and UNICEF in resource mobilisation, technology innovation and public diplomacy.

Jan Böhm is a digital strategist at Médecins sans Frontières/Doctors Without Borders (MSF). He focuses on the use of digital tools for communication and collaboration. Between 2016 and 2019, he worked as a community engagement manager for Missing Maps in MSF. In this role, he supported Missing Maps communities facilitated by MSF in over twenty countries from Argentina to Zimbabwe. He has led trainings for MSF mapathon organisers in Beirut, Dubai, Singapore and Prague.

Juliana Guarany da Cunha Santos is a Brazilian journalist. After working for fifteen years in newsrooms in Brazil, she was selected as a fellow from the Alexander von Humboldt Foundation to develop FemMap in Germany, where she currently lives.

Leah Temper is an ecological economist and political ecologist. She is a research associate at McGill University for the Leadership for the Ecozoic program and co-founder and director of the Global Atlas of Environmental Justice (www.ejatlas.org). She is also a mother, filmmaker and rabble-rouser.

Lena Weber is currently a PhD student based at the Institute of Environmental Science and Technology (ICTA), Autonomous University of Barcelona, Catalunya, Spain. Lena spent the last decade working in and studying youth engagement, critical cartography, environmental conflicts, digital and physical security of activists under surveillance and the relationships between systemic oppression, climate change, academia and diverse and creative forms of resistance.

Noora Flinkman is the technology lead at HarassMap and manages the development and deployment of its crowdmapping platform. She previously headed HarassMap's marketing and communications team in Egypt.

Nooreen Reza was a founding member of the Intolerance Tracker team while at the University of Cambridge. She currently attends the law school at the University of Virginia in the US, where she focuses on economic inequality and housing justice.

Rebecca Chiao is HarassMap's co-founder and board member. She holds an MA in International Development and Economics (Johns Hopkins SAIS), a certificate in Strategic Frameworks for NGOs (Harvard KSG) and a BA in politics (NYU), and has worked at the Egyptian Centre for Women's Rights, Ashoka Arab World and INJAZ Egypt.

Rebecca Rumbul holds a PhD in politics and governance, and leads mySociety's research team, conducting rigorous global research projects supporting evidence-based development of policy and practice around digital tools for participation, transparency and accountability. Rebecca has extensive international fieldwork experience at the intersection of development, digital technology and democracy. She has worked with parliaments to better understand how they manage information and the benefits of adopting a more transparent approach, enhance their ability to produce, manage and release open data and identify pathways for ongoing improvement of data and digital systems.

Rob Shepard is Assistant Professor of Geography at the University of Nebraska–Lincoln. He researches human–environment issues in the American Great Plains as well as historical and contemporary geographic disparities relating to ethnicity, class and gender. He was previously the Geographic Information Systems (GIS) specialist at the University of Iowa's Digital Scholarship and Publishing Studio.

Sandhya Christabel D'Souza currently works as an associate at Citizen Communications, Janaagraha Centre for Citizenship and Democracy.

Shannon Mattern is Professor at The New School for Social Research, New York. Her writing and teaching focus on media architectures and infrastructures and spatial epistemologies. She has written books about libraries, maps and the history of urban intelligence. She contributes a column to *Places Journal*. You can find her at wordsinspace.net.

Sumit Arora is currently working as the head of Civic Tech Platforms at Janaagraha Centre for Citizenship and Democracy.

Taha Kass-Hout is a cardiologist and bioinformatician, who served two terms in the US federal government: as the first chief health informatics officer for US FDA (2013–2016) and at the US CDC for electronic disease surveillance (2009–2013). He is also the founder of Humanitarian Tracker, which uses crowdsourcing to map the spread of disease and disasters such as the current crisis in Syria.